THE FORGOTTEN FEAR

THE FORGOTTEN FEAR

WHERE HAVE ALL THE
GOD-FEARERS GONE?

Albert N. Martin

REFORMATION HERITAGE BOOKS
Grand Rapids, Michigan

Reformation Heritage Books
2965 Leonard St. NE
Grand Rapids, MI 49525
616-977-0889 / Fax 616-285-3246
orders@heritagebooks.org
www.heritagebooks.org

Printed in the United States of America
15 16 17 18 19 20/10 9 8 7 6 5 4 3 2 1

Library of Congress Cataloging-in-Publication Data

Martin, Albert N.
  The forgotten fear : where have all the God-fearers gone? / Albert N. Martin.
      pages cm
  Includes bibliographical references.
  ISBN 978-1-60178-421-6 (pbk. : alk. paper) 1. Fear of God—Biblical teaching. 2. Fear of God—Christianity. I. Title.
  BS680.F42M37 2015
  231.7—dc23
                              2015031679

For additional Reformed literature, request a free book list from Reformation Heritage Books at the above regular or e-mail address.

Contents

Foreword

When in the late 1960s Al Martin arrived in England and spoke at the Banner of Truth Conference, there was an immediate recognition that this was a new and powerful voice declaring in a winsome and moving way the old truths. Dr. Martin was like a man who had dug a hole in a field and discovered treasure. He had read Ryle and Murray, Warfield and M'Cheyne, the Reformers, the Puritans, the leaders of the Evangelical Awakening, Spurgeon, Tozer, and Lloyd-Jones, and he had made them his own. He declared them not in a copycat way, not in mere word, but in power and in the Holy Spirit and with much assurance. He refreshed and quickened us so that we who heard him were encouraged to examine again those past leaders of the mighty works of God and ask the reason for the impact they made in their generation.

There are several marks of the blessing of God on a ministry. Many people are converted, new assurance is given to Christian believers, and the fear of the Lord is present in that place. That is a basic Christian response to the gospel preached and lived out by the followers of the Lord Jesus from the very beginning. Hear this refrain from the book of Acts: "So great fear came on all those who heard these things" (Acts 5:5); "Great fear came upon all the church" (Acts 5:11). "Then the churches throughout all Judea, Galilee, and Samaria had peace and were edified. And walking in the fear of the Lord and in the comfort of the Holy Spirit, they were multiplied" (Acts 9:31). "Fear fell on them all, and the name of the Lord Jesus was magnified" (Acts 19:17). So the New Testament church at its most vibrant and credible lived its life "throughout the time of [its] stay here in fear" (1 Peter 1:17).

The solemn distinctive of a world that has rejected Christ is, "There is no fear of God before their eyes" (Rom. 3:18), while the voice from heaven addresses the world, crying out, "Fear God and give glory to Him" (Rev. 14:7). Fearing God is not some option for a few special Christians. It is foundational to all who name God as their God—an utterly essential mark of true religion. A stranger to the fear of God is a stranger to the living God Himself. This grace must characterize all true Christian worship under the blessing of God.

How we need help here, and this book of Dr. Martin is one valuable means of kindling the flame of the fear of God in the midst of the church again. It began in a series of sermons preached in his church and then to gatherings of Christians. Always the messages enlightened, convicted, and motivated the hearers. There was thanksgiving, praise, and a new determination to walk in the fear of God. Dr. Martin has carefully worked on this material, keeping the immediacy of the preaching style without its necessary redundancies, but maintaining its engagement and application, addressing the consciences of all who read these pages, and enlightening the mind with careful biblical exegesis. I thank God for this means of grace and commend it to you. May our generation cry out, "Who shall not fear You, O Lord?" (Rev. 15:4).

—Geoff Thomas

CHAPTER ONE

Predominance of the Fear of God in Biblical Thought

The fear of God is a massive and dominant theme in Scripture. It is also a theme that was very prominent both in the thinking and in the preaching of our spiritual forefathers. When our spiritual forefathers desired to describe someone who was characterized by genuine godliness, they would often call him a "God-fearing man." This designation reflected the fact that men realized the fear of God was nothing less than the soul of godliness. Take away the soul from the body, and all you have left in a few days is a stinking carcass. Take away the fear of God from any profession of godliness, and all that is left is the stinking carcass of pharisaism, barren religiosity, or calculated hypocrisy.

To begin, let us consider the predominance of the fear of God in biblical thought. One does not need much learning to reach the conclusion that the fear of God is indeed a dominant theme in the Bible. In fact, equipped with a relatively good concordance (such as Strong's or Young's), you could discover the major concerns of the study that I am here presenting. If you looked up the word "fear" in your concordance, you would notice that there are no fewer than

150 to 175 explicit references to the fear of God. If you add to these explicit references the instances in Scripture where the fear of God is illustrated, though not explicitly stated, it is accurate to say that the references to the fear of God run well into the hundreds. It is amazing, then, that a theme so dominant in the Old and the New Testaments can either be greatly overlooked or carelessly treated, as it often is in our day. I trust after we grasp something of the predominance of this theme that you will not be content with a mere cursory knowledge or passing acquaintance with the fear of God. One simply cannot claim to love the God and truths of the Bible and still remain indifferent to a subject which is so prominent throughout the Scripture.[1]

The Fear of God in the Old Testament
We start first with an overview of the fear of God in the Old Testament.

The Books of the Law
Genesis 31 is perhaps one of the most significant passages in all of Scripture as it relates to the predominance of the fear of God in biblical thought. Here, the patriarch Jacob said, "Unless the God of my father, the God of Abraham and the Fear of Isaac, had been with me, surely now you would have sent me away empty-handed" (v. 42). Throughout the

---

1. For an excellent summary of the primary Hebrew and Greek words used to express the concept of "fear," consult the footnotes on pages 231–32 in John Murray, *Principles of Conduct: Aspects of Biblical Ethics* (Grand Rapids: Eerdmans, 1957).

Scriptures, God's name is a revelation of His character. Here, one of His names is "the Fear of Isaac." When God is rightly apprehended, true biblical fear of Him is so much a part of a right response to the revelation of His character that He calls Himself "the Fear of Isaac." If my perception of God and my comprehension of His revealed character do not lead me to fear Him as Isaac did, I have not rightly understood who God is.

Exodus 18 contains the record of Moses' problem of seeking to govern single-handedly the entire nation of Israel, including dealing with many concerns that called for the judgment of a mature mind. Jethro, his father-in-law, suggested that Moses was not up to the task by himself and that he ought to share this oversight with other competent men. When the requirements are given for those who would qualify to fill this role as judges, verse 21 says, "Moreover you shall select from all the people able men, such as fear God, men of truth, hating covetousness; and place such over them to be rulers of thousands, rulers of hundreds, rulers of fifties, and rulers of tens." Of all the requirements that could be laid down for men to administer justice in the mighty nation which Israel had become, set at the very pinnacle of importance is that they must be men who fear God. Whatever other qualities they may or may not have, if they are not men whose primary characteristic is the fear of God, they would not be qualified for this significant role of administering justice and solving problems within the nation of Israel.

In Deuteronomy 4, Moses explains to the nation of Israel why God had chosen to give them His laws and statutes. Moses charges the nation not to forget the words God spoke to them, "that they may learn to fear Me all the days they live on the earth, and that they may teach their children" (v. 12). In this passage, God Himself indicates that the great end for which He made known His words to the nation of Israel was that they might learn what it means to fear God.

When the apostle Paul is enumerating the peculiar privileges the nation had, he asserts, "What advantage then has the Jew, or what is the profit of circumcision? Much in every way! Chiefly because to them were committed the oracles of God" (Rom. 3:2). If the chief blessing of being an Israelite was being a possessor of God's words, and God Himself says that those words were given to teach them to fear Him, then the fear of God is a central motif in the entire corpus of the Mosaic revelation.

The Book of Job

In the book of Job, we shift from God's dealings to teach an entire nation His fear to His dealings with an individual Old Testament saint. This saint is not like the Pharisee who boasted of his own supposed attainments in grace, but one of whom God Himself boasts. The book begins with these words: "There was a man in the land of Uz, whose name was Job; and that man was blameless and upright, and one who feared God and shunned evil" (Job 1:1). The words "blameless and upright" constitute a description of the observable patterns of Job's life. However, God goes on to describe the inward disposition that produced those patterns. Job is "one who *feared God.*" This identification of the outward patterns and the inward principle of Job's life is repeated in verse 8, "Then the LORD said to Satan, 'Have you considered My servant Job, that there is none like him on the earth, a blameless and upright man, one who fears God and shuns evil?'" The soul of Job's external piety was this inward fear of his God. Verse 9 reads, "So Satan answered the LORD and said, 'Does Job fear God for nothing?'" Satan responds that God believes that the fear of His name is the soul of Job's godliness, but Job has another dominant and self-serving motive for the service he renders to Him. The whole story then unfolds as God vindicates His claims on behalf of His servant Job. But we see that the essence of Job's piety—and God's estimation of all true piety—is that it is animated by and suffused with the fear of God.

The Psalms

As we observe the central place the Old Testament gives to the fear of God, we look next at the Psalms. Here we will find many references to the fear of God. In Psalm 2, God reveals His purpose to exalt His Son to His messianic throne from which He will execute both grace and judgment. Having announced that purpose, God then gives the following command:

> Now therefore, be wise, O kings;
> Be instructed, you judges of the earth.
> Serve the LORD with fear,
> And rejoice with trembling. (Ps. 2:10–11)

God is saying, "In the light of what I have purposed to do with reference to My Son and the pivotal place which

I have assigned to Him, the only right response is service rendered to Him that is carried out in the context of godly fear." "Serve the LORD with fear." We must say, then, that if our view of Christ and His exaltation by the Father's decree does not induce us to serve Him in the climate of godly fear, we have not rightly understood nor responded to the exaltation of the Son by the decree of the Father.

Psalm 67 is one of those great gospel psalms that focuses on the proclamation of God's saving mercy to the ends of the earth. The psalmist pleads that God will be merciful to him and to His covenant people—to this end: "That Your way may be known on earth, Your salvation among all nations" (Ps. 67:2). And what will be the result of God's saving message going out to the nations? The answer is in verse 7: "God shall bless us, and all the ends of the earth shall fear Him." In other words, the whole end for which the gospel goes out through God's covenant people is to teach the nations the fear of God. Does this not make the fear of God a most crucial issue in our understanding and experience of God's salvation? God expresses His determination to bless His people in order that they in turn may bring blessing to others. He states His purpose in these words: "God shall bless us, and all the ends of the earth shall fear Him" (v. 7).

Psalm 103 contains several references to the fear of God, and they have a common thread. They teach us that the fear of God is an indispensable characteristic of the true people of God. So much is this the case, that in describing the true people of God, the psalmist uses this phrase— those who *fear God*. Notice verse 11: "For as the heavens are high above the earth, so great is His mercy toward those who fear Him." Does it say that His mercy is toward all men? No. The idea that God's redemptive love is just some kind of a general, gushy benevolence that is focused on all men without distinction is not the teaching of Holy Scripture. Here the psalmist says, "His mercy [is] toward *those who fear Him*." His peculiar love is on His people. And who are His people, but those who fear Him? If there is no fear of Him, there is no steadfast mercy resting upon us or exercised toward us. Verse 13 makes a similar assertion: "As a father pities his children, so the LORD pities those who fear Him." God's "children" are parallel to "those who fear Him." This means that if I have no fear of God, I have no right to claim that I am under the canopy of redemptive love (v. 11), and no right to claim that I am one of His children (v. 13; cf. v. 17). The psalmist conceives of the people of God as those who are in every instance marked by this characteristic of the fear of God.

The Writings of Solomon

Proverbs 1 is another important text regarding the fear of God, especially verse 7. In the first six verses, Solomon introduces Proverbs as a textbook full of wise counsels with a manifold purpose. Then, as he begins to lay out the path to the attainment of knowledge and wisdom, he makes this statement at the very beginning of his discourse: "The fear of the LORD is the beginning of knowledge, but fools despise wisdom and instruction" (v. 7). In other words, learning the fear of God is not only the ABCs from which we move on to the rest of the alphabet. Learning the fear of God is not like learning to spell the word "cat"—one of the first words we learn to spell—and then moving on while acquiring the ability to spell the word "disestablishmentarianism." Rather, the fear of God is the *chief part*, just as the use of the alphabet is something that is not left behind but becomes the chief part of all our learning. Thus, when a man is studying the most complicated book on physics, he is dependent on the same numbers and letters he learned in kindergarten and first grade. Now the physics book may contain complex arrangements of those letters and numbers, but the physicist works with the same letters and numbers he learned as a four- or five-year-old. In the same way, the fear of the Lord is the chief part of knowledge. It is not only the beginning but that which permeates all accumulation of heavenly knowledge at every point along the way. Without the presence of that fear, God says there is no true wisdom. The fear of the Lord is the beginning of knowledge.

Then we turn to the book of Ecclesiastes, and we hear the insights of a man (Solomon) who surveyed all the possible avenues down which a man may go to find meaning and satisfaction in life. You may have contemplated going down some of those paths that seem so inviting and promise so much, as they did to this man in the beginning. But as he went down to the end of every one of those paths, he saw that they were nothing but vanity and vexation, until he came to the conclusion couched in the last verses of the last chapter: "Let us hear the conclusion of the whole matter: Fear God, and keep his commandments: for this is the whole duty of man. For God shall bring every work into judgment, with every secret thing, whether it be good, or whether it be evil" (Eccl. 12:13–14).

While this concluding statement does not address God's gracious provision for sinners who universally do not fear God by nature (Rom. 3:18), it does clearly identify the fear of God as central to our duty as creatures made in the image of God.

The Prophets

In Isaiah 11:1–2, we have a beautiful prophecy of the Messiah who would come out of the stock of Jesse:

> There shall come forth a Rod from the stem of Jesse,
> And a Branch shall grow out of his roots.
> The Spirit of the LORD shall rest upon Him,
> The Spirit of wisdom and understanding,
> The Spirit of counsel and might,
> The Spirit of knowledge and of the fear of the LORD.

Here is an explicit statement that the Spirit would come on Messiah, as the Spirit did in fact come on Him in conjunction with His baptism in the waters of Jordan. Isaiah says the Spirit would come on Him not only as the Spirit of might and of power by which He raised the dead, unstopped deafened ears, and loosened dumb tongues, but that He would rest on Him as the "Spirit of the fear of the Lord." That fact is the one aspect of the Spirit's ministry which is enlarged upon in verse 3: "His delight is in the fear of the LORD." The prophet foretells that the dominant aspect of Messiah's own character is that He would live and move and delight in the fear of the Lord.

This fact should immediately purge from our minds any notion that the fear of God is incompatible with an assured sense of God's favor. It was in the very context of empowering our Lord with the Spirit ("the Spirit of the fear of the LORD") that the Father audibly expressed His delight in Jesus as His beloved Son.

In Jeremiah 32, Jeremiah speaks of the new covenant, a covenant that we know from other Scriptures would be brought into effect by the sufferings and death of our Lord Jesus Christ. This is the covenant sealed and ratified by the blood of Christ as expounded in Hebrews 8 and 10. Notice what God says will happen when the blessings of the new covenant are brought to men: "They shall be My people, and I will be their God; then I will give them one heart and one way, that they may fear Me forever, for the good of them and their children after them. And I will make an everlasting covenant with them, that I will not turn away from doing them good; but I will put My fear in their hearts so that they will not depart from Me" (Jer. 32:38–40).

God says, in effect, "The whole end for which I will work in such power in this new covenant is to put My fear within the hearts of My people so that they will not turn away from Me." According to this passage, it is the fear of God placed in the hearts of the beneficiaries of the new covenant that becomes the principal reason for their perseverance in faith, and in a loving and obedient attachment to the God of their salvation.

Do you believe that you are a recipient of the blessings of the new covenant? Do you frequent the Lord's Table, where you take the outward symbols of the blood of that covenant? God says that if you have inwardly partaken of the benefits of that covenant, one of the dominant characteristics of your life will be that you now live in the fear of God. If you are a stranger to that fear, then you are a stranger to the blessings of the new covenant. You are yet in your sins. You are still under the wrath of Almighty God. Every time the benefits of the new covenant are applied with power by the Spirit, God says they are applied in such a way that He puts His fear in the heart. The fear of God is a central theme of the new covenant itself.

It is true that under God's previous covenants, every elect sinner was regenerated and indwelt by the Holy Spirit, received a justifying righteousness, and experienced the blessing of having the fear of God implanted in his heart. It is this fact alone that explains the godly patterns of life attributed to Old Testament believers. Furthermore, we know from the overall teachings of Scripture that any and all saving benefits in every stage of redemptive history have been given to guilty and depraved sinners on the basis of the work of Christ as the only Mediator of sinners. Yet it is only within the terms of the new covenant that this blessing is explicitly guaranteed to all those who are brought to repentance and faith in the context of the accomplished salvation proclaimed in the new covenant (Jer. 32:40).

In the light of this handful of references taken from scores of others in the Old Testament, we must conclude that the fear of God, whatever it is, is a predominant theme in the Old Testament. It is not an optional virtue but absolutely essential and central in God's saving work.

The Fear of God in the New Testament

But we can imagine someone objecting, "Yes, but the texts you have cited are part of the dark and shadowy religion of the Old Testament. We now have the full revelation of God's love and mercy in Jesus Christ in the New Testament. Just as the types and shadows of the blood of bulls and goats have been fulfilled in Christ, so has that dark, foreboding concept of the fear of God given way to the bright and breezy quality of the joy of the Lord." Is that true? Let us see whether the New Testament itself will support such thinking.

The Gospels

What do we find as we turn to the New Testament? Shortly after the Lord Jesus was conceived in His mother's womb, Mary visited her cousin Elizabeth. Upon her arrival at the home of Zacharias and Elizabeth, Mary was filled with the Spirit, and she spoke those words of prophetic praise commonly called the Magnificat. In this Spirit-inspired poem of praise, Mary testified that she saw in God's dealings with her an illustration of a principle that had characterized God's dealings with His people throughout the centuries— one that would characterize His dealings with His people through the very One she now carried in her womb. Mary saw that what God was doing simply illustrated what He had always done with His people—and what He will continue to do through the coming of the Son of God. Here is her testimony: "For He who is mighty has done great things for me, and holy is His name. And His mercy is on those who fear Him from generation to generation" (Luke 1:49–50). God's way is to show mercy to those who fear Him.

Mary saw God's mercy to her as illustrating this principle, a principle that will continue to operate as Messiah comes and carries out His mission. Here then, in one of the opening chapters of the gospel records, God makes it unmistakably clear that His true people have been and remain characterized as those who "fear Him."

What did our Lord Himself teach? Certainly, if He wanted men not to fear God but simply to have joy in and love for God, we would expect to find Him discouraging anything like fear, especially anything that had the fear of dread in it. As we will see in our more formal definition, there are two basic aspects of the fear of God, as in all human fear. There is dread, and there is awe. The first aspect of fear drives us *from* the object of dread; the other aspect draws us *to* the object of awe. Our Lord's teaching makes very clear that both aspects are included in a healthy fear of God—including this element of dread. While commissioning the twelve disciples, He first warns them not to fear what men can do to them. He says, "And do not fear those who kill the body but cannot kill the soul. But rather fear Him who is able to destroy both soul and body in hell" (Matt. 10:28). Jesus was not on a mission to do away with the fear of God. Instead He enforced it by *commanding* His disciples to possess in their breasts the fear that even includes the element of dread—fear of what God would do if they were to fall into His hands with their sins laid to their charge. As the writer to the Hebrews reminds us, it is indeed "a fearful thing to fall into the hands of the living God" (Heb. 10:31). Jesus did not come to negate the fear of God; He came to enforce it. We shall see in our further studies that, as there were grounds in the shadowy revelation of God in the old covenant to fear Him, so the fuller revelation in the new covenant has only intensified the obligation of godly fear.

The Book of Acts

In the early chapters of Acts, Luke describes the maturity of the early church and God's blessing on her. Notice how two things are fused together beautifully. Though we would separate them, God brings them together. Following the conversion of Saul, who had made havoc of the church, we read in Acts 9:31, "Then the churches throughout all Judea, Galilee, and Samaria had peace and were edified. And walking in the fear of the Lord and in the comfort of the Holy Spirit, they were multiplied." We tend to think that wherever there is the Spirit's comfort, there is no fear of God; and if there is the fear of God, then there will be no Spirit's comfort. But that is not the case at all. The Spirit that rested on Christ, the Spirit whom He received in plentitude and now Himself pours out on His church, is "the Spirit of the fear of the LORD" (Isa. 11:2). And just as the fear of the Lord characterized Jesus Himself, so the more His church is filled with the Spirit of Jesus, the more that church will also live, worship, and witness in the fear of the Lord. John Murray writes:

> If he who was holy, harmless, undefiled, and separate from sinners was endued with the Spirit of the Fear of the Lord, how can thought or feeling that is not conditioned by God's fear have any kinship with him who is the captain of our salvation and who has given

us an example that we should follow in his steps? The church walks in the fear of the Lord because the Spirit of Christ indwells, fills, directs, and rests upon the church and the Spirit of Christ is the Spirit of the fear of the Lord.[2]

The Epistles

Now we turn to the epistles of the New Testament. Paul wrote in 2 Corinthians 7:1, "Therefore, having these promises, beloved, let us cleanse ourselves from all filthiness of the flesh and spirit, perfecting holiness in the fear of God." Is there remaining sin to be dealt with in the life of a believer? Is he expected, on the one hand, to mortify the deeds of the flesh, and, on the other, to cultivate every grace that will bring him into greater conformity to Jesus Christ? Every properly instructed Christian says, "Yes, but how are we to do this?" Are we to think primarily that the more holy we are, the more gracious rewards we will receive when we stand before the Lord? Or, the more we are filled with the Spirit, the more joy and happiness and peace and vibrancy we'll have? There is certainly an element of truth in both these things, but I suggest that neither is to be our primary focus. According to Paul's words in 2 Corinthians 7:1, the highest reaches of attainment in practical holiness and godliness are to be achieved and sought after in the climate of the fear of God.

If the fear of God is the climate in which we are to pursue practical godliness, what constitutes a major area of

---

2. Murray, *Principles of Conduct*, 230.

concern in the attainment of practical godliness? It is how we conduct ourselves in our interpersonal relationships. Much of the specific and detailed ethical instruction found in the Sermon on the Mount and the Epistles is focused on various interpersonal relationships. The "godliness" that leaves you nasty with your boss, churlish with your wife, bossy with your husband, or snippy with your mom and dad is no godliness at all. The godliness and holiness of the Bible are intensely practical things that show up most clearly in the interactions with your deepest and most intimate human relationships, whether in the family, work, church, or school. Our holiness, our progress in sanctification, must be seen in those relationships. As we pursue greater degrees of holiness in those relationships, what is to constitute a dominant motive in that pursuit?

In Ephesians 5:21 and following, Paul addresses the various relationships in a household—the husband-wife relationship, the parent-child relationship, and the master-slave relationship. Notice what he says to introduce these domestic concerns in verse 21: "submitting to one another in the fear of God." All of these commands that speak about the nitty-gritty of practical godliness in matters of interpersonal relationships are couched in the framework of the fear of God. Therefore, any attempt to progress in holiness in these relationships that ignores this idea of the fear of God is something less (if not something totally other) than that which is set before us in the Word of God.

In Philippians 2:12–13, Paul commands believers to work out their salvation: "Therefore, my beloved, as you have always obeyed, not as in my presence only, but now much more in my absence, work out your own salvation with fear and trembling; for it is God who works in you both to will and to do for His good pleasure." What is the context of that working out of our salvation? It is to be one characterized by "fear and trembling." In light of these words, what biblical truths have given birth to the current notion that a laid-back, cavalier, and sprightly attitude constitute the essence of advanced spirituality? What biblical truths have persuaded many professing Christians that serious, self-denying discipleship is the essence of legalism? Paul's prescription is that our salvation is to be worked out in a climate of godly "fear and trembling." Anyone who is working out his salvation without this disposition is working it out in a context unauthorized by the Word of God. What "fear and trembling" is will be explained further on in the book. But at this juncture, suffice it to say that this "fear and trembling" is to be a dominant characteristic in the life of every true Christian who is committed to "working out his salvation."

But does this have to continue all throughout the Christian's life? Can't we come to a place where we no longer need the various constraints of the fear of God? Let the apostle Peter answer that question. We have looked at Jesus' words and the apostle Paul's. Peter gives the same word. And he speaks of it in a most interesting context. He says in 1 Peter 1:17–19, "And if you call on the Father, who without partiality judges according to each one's work, conduct yourselves throughout the time of your stay here in fear; knowing that you were not redeemed with corruptible things, like silver or gold, from your aimless conduct received by tradition from your fathers, but with the precious blood of Christ, as of a lamb without blemish and without spot." The question could be raised, but if one possesses a well-grounded biblical assurance that one has been saved by the blood of Christ, shouldn't this negate any fear of God? No, it should not, because Peter says in the next verse: "knowing that you were not redeemed with corruptible things, like silver or gold." He says the knowledge that you have been redeemed at such an awful price will intensify the reality of the fear of God, not negate it. He uses the fact that *we know we have been redeemed by the precious blood of Christ* as his very argument to enforce the necessity of walking in godly fear, and that we must pass the whole time of our exile in fear. At every point in my Christian life, from the moment I breathe my first breath as a new creature in Christ to the moment when I take my last breath, the entire time of my sojourning—all of this is to be marked by the fear of God.

The Book of Revelation

The fear of God is so fundamental to godliness that even into eternity, even after the last remains of sin are purged from believers, we will still fear God. Our last two references are taken from Revelation. The first is found in Revelation 15. Here, in graphic language, we have set before us a picture of the redeemed of God in verses 2–4:

> And I saw something like a sea of glass mingled with fire, and those who have the victory over the beast, over his image and over his mark and over the number of his name, standing on the sea of glass, having

harps of God. They sing the song of Moses, the servant of God, and the song of the Lamb, saying:

"Great and marvelous are Your works,
Lord God Almighty!
Just and true are Your ways,
O King of the saints!
Who shall not fear You, O Lord,
    and glorify Your name?
For You alone are holy.
For all nations shall come and worship before You,
For Your judgments have been manifested."

In the light of the marvel of His works and the righteousness of His ways, what should be the response of the redeemed there in His presence? Verse 4 gives the answer: "Who shall not fear You, O Lord, and glorify Your name?" The fear of God will mark the worship of the redeemed, even when they are glorified and are worshiping in God's immediate presence.

Similar words of praise are recorded in Revelation 19:4–5: "And the twenty-four elders and the four living creatures fell down and worshiped God who sat on the throne, saying, 'Amen! Alleluia!' Then a voice came from the throne, saying, 'Praise our God, all you His servants and those who fear Him, both small and great!'"

How does the Spirit describe the redeemed in the context of a fully realized redemption? They are characterized as "those who fear Him." Their fear of God is singled out as the prominent identifying characteristic of the servants of God.

Conclusions from the Biblical Evidence

What can we conclude in light of these pivotal texts found in both the Old and the New Testaments? First, I believe we are warranted to conclude that *to be devoid of the fear of God is to be devoid of biblical and saving religion.* It matters not how many texts of Scripture we can quote, or how many promises we may claim to believe. In the light of the texts of Scripture we have briefly considered (and they are but a sampling of many more), it is neither unkind nor unjust to assert that if you do not know what the fear of God is in your heart and life, you do not know experientially the first thing about true biblical and saving religion. That is a serious conclusion, but no less a conclusion can be drawn from these passages. Since Jesus Christ is the sum and substance of biblical religion, and since the Spirit given to Him and sent from Him is the Spirit of the fear of God, to be without the fear of God is to be without the Spirit of Christ. Romans 8:9 says that those without the Spirit of Christ do not belong to Christ. If such teaching is utterly foreign to you and leaves you completely baffled, you need to engage in some serious reflection. You need to examine the Scriptures and cry out to God, asking Him to teach you what it is to fear Him, for you see that if you are devoid of His fear, you have no true saving religion.

The second conclusion we are warranted in making is this: *one of the accurate measurements of true spiritual growth is the measure to which one increases in walking in the fear of God.* The Bible speaks of Hananiah in Nehemiah 7:2 as a man who "feared God more than many." His spiritual stature as a man who possessed spiritual maturity, wisdom, and godliness to an exceptional degree was in great measure due to the fact that he "feared God more than many."

Third, *to be ignorant of the meaning of the fear of God is to be ignorant of a basic and essential doctrine of revealed religion.* There are no doubt many in our day who are genuine Christians yet who are sadly deficient in their understanding of the concept of the fear of God. They are not strangers to the fear of God in their experience, but they are very unclear about the fear of God in their understanding. Are you such a Christian? Has your reading of this book thus far been like walking on ground unfamiliar to you? Since growth in grace is always joined to growth in knowledge (2 Peter 3:18), it is vital to give yourself to earnest prayer and study so that you might have a clearer understanding of the fear of God. This, in turn, will lead to your further Christian growth and development.[3]

---

3. For any readers who desire a clearer understanding of the fear of God, see chapter 10 in John Murray's *Principles of Conduct*, John Bunyan's *The Fear of God*, and Arnold L. Frank's *The Fear of God*—the latter being a most helpful collection of teaching on the fear of God drawn primarily from Puritan authors.

Questions for Reflection and Discussion

1. What numerical facts demonstrate the predominance of this subject of the fear of God in the Scriptures?

2. In what ways is the fear of God taught and illustrated in the Pentateuch?

3. What significance did the fear of God have in the life of Job?

4. How is the fear of God presented to us in the Psalms and the other parts of the Wisdom Literature of the Old Testament?

5. Where and how does Isaiah describe the place of the fear of God in the experience of the coming Messiah? In what way should this influence your life?

6. What passages in Jeremiah highlight the place of the fear of God in the new covenant?

7. Identify at least five key texts from the Gospels to Revelation which conclusively prove that the fear of God is not an exclusively Old Testament emphasis.

CHAPTER TWO

---------- ◆ ----------

Definition of the Fear of God

"The fear of God is the soul of godliness."[1] Yet observant Christians see that this pervasive and dominant theme of Holy Scripture has nearly been lost to many in this generation. As we endeavor to acquaint ourselves with at least some of the pivotal aspects of the scriptural teaching on this subject, I sought to do but one thing in the first chapter—to help the reader to capture and feel something of the predominance of the fear of God in biblical thought.

Now let us consider the meaning of the fear of God as defined by Scripture. It is one thing to feel the weight Scripture gives this concept. It is another thing to make sure we draw from that concept the meaning that Scripture demands. How do we discover how to define the fear of God according to Scripture? Since God used two Hebrew words and one Greek word for fear when describing the fear of God, we will simply begin by finding out how the word "fear" is defined by its general usage in Scripture.

---

1. Murray, *Principles of Conduct*, 229.

Then we will see how the two facets of its general usage have been incorporated into its meaning when it refers to the fear of God.

The Word "Fear" in Its General Biblical Usage

How is the word "fear" used in the everyday language of Scripture? First is the fear that can be described as experiencing <u>terror or dread</u>. It is the kind of fear a nine-year-old boy feels when he is walking home from school, turns the corner, and sees the neighborhood bully standing in the middle of the sidewalk. There stands a fourteen-year-old kid who is five feet ten inches tall who loves to beat up little nine-year-olds who are only four feet tall. When this little nine-year-old turns the corner and sees the bully, who looks like a giant to him, suddenly he is gripped with terror and dread. That terror is based on the recognition of the potential harm that the bully can do to him.

The word "fear" in biblical usage sometimes describes this kind of fear. It is used this way in Deuteronomy 2, beginning with verse 24. God gives a command to His people, saying, "Rise, take your journey, and cross over the River Arnon. Look, I have given into your hand Sihon the Amorite, king of Heshbon, and his land. Begin to possess it, and engage him in battle. This day I will begin to put the dread and fear of you upon the nations under the whole heaven, who shall hear the report of you, and shall tremble and be in anguish because of you" (vv. 24–25).

In these verses God is telling His people that the Canaanites will fear them. They will be filled with terror or dread because He will lend His presence and power to

His people to make them mighty in battle. The Canaanites will be filled with terror, with anguish. The word used here in verse 25 is the same word that refers to the fear of God.

There is a similar reference in Psalm 105:36–38. Speaking of the deliverance by which God brought His people out of Egypt, we read, "He also destroyed all the firstborn in their land, the first of all their strength. He also brought them out with silver and gold, and there was none feeble among His tribes. Egypt was glad when they departed, for the fear of them had fallen upon them." That is, they had begun to dread the presence of the Israelites because of the terrible judgments the God of the Israelites inflicted on the Egyptians. This again is the fear of dread and terror.

There is an example of this in the New Testament in the familiar Christmas passage. We read in Luke 2:9 that when the angels suddenly appeared to the shepherds, the shepherds were terrified. "They were greatly afraid" (Luke 2:9). Their fear at the presence of the angels in this unusual manifestation was the fear of dread. One other reference in the New Testament is Acts 5:11. When the news went out concerning how God struck Ananias and Sapphira dead because of their attempts to lie to the Holy Spirit, Scripture tells us that "great fear came upon all the church and upon all who heard these things." Thus, in both the Old and the New Testaments, this common word "fear" is used to describe the emotion of being gripped with terror and dread.

But there is another kind of fear. The same word is used for this second kind of fear, but it is used with an obviously different meaning. It is the fear of veneration and honor, the fear of respect or awe. Consider that same

nine-year-old boy referred to earlier. He is no longer turning the corner on his way home and confronting the town
bully, but he is now with his schoolmates. They have taken
a class trip and gone to Washington, D.C. As they walk
through the various parts of the White House on a guided
tour, suddenly an official breaks into the ranks and says to
this young boy, "The president of the United States wishes
to talk with you." Immediately the boy's eyes open wide, his
breath begins to come hard, and he stammers, "He wants
to talk to me?" "Yes, to you; your name is Billy Jones, isn't
it?" The boy is filled with fear. But this fear is not the fear of
dread. He is not afraid that the president is going to issue
an order that will bring soldiers out to hold rifles to his
head. No, his fear is the fear that comes when an individual
stands in the presence of someone who is superior in worth
and dignity. It is the fear of veneration, honor, and awe.

Now notice how this aspect of the word "fear" is captured in a text such as Leviticus 19:3: "Every one of you shall
revere his mother and his father, and keep My Sabbaths:
I am the LORD your God." Is God commanding children
that, every time they look at their mother and father, they
are to have the same feeling that comes over them when
they meet the neighborhood bully? Does He want them,
whenever they see Mom and Dad, to shake in their shoes?
Of course not. But He says they should *fear* their parents.
The same word is used, but it has a very different meaning. God is saying to children that they are to recognize in
their father and mother not just individuals who are taller,
bigger, wiser, and a bit more experienced. They are to recognize that, because they are their father and mother, they

are God's representatives to administer His rule and will to them. Therefore, because of the dignity of their position, children are to regard their parents with veneration, honor, and awe. This is not the fear of dread and terror.

These two common uses of the word "fear" in the vocabulary of the people of biblical times (and also in some measure in our vocabulary) are both included in the biblical notion of the fear of God. There is a legitimate sense in which the fear of God involves *being afraid of God, being gripped with terror and dread.* Though this is not the dominant thought in Scripture, it is there nonetheless. The second aspect of fear, which is peculiar to the true children of God, *is the fear of veneration, honor, and awe with which we regard our God.* It is a fear that leads us not to run from Him but to draw near to Him through Jesus Christ and gladly submit to Him in faith, love, and obedience.

Since common words for fear are used in both the Old and New Testaments, a careful examination of the context of the various uses is essential in order to discern whether the fear spoken of in any given passage of Scripture is the fear of dread and terror or the fear of reverential awe, veneration, and honor, or, both kinds together (as it appears in a few instances).

The Fear of Dread and Terror
Old Testament Witness

Let us first consider the fear of dread or terror—the fear that leads to anguish and an aversion to its object. The first recorded instance of any fear of God is this kind of fear. The setting is the garden of Eden, where God had placed Adam in a perfect environment and surrounded him with everything that Adam's holy nature could desire. God had issued the threat to Adam that if he ate of that one forbidden tree, in that day he would die. After Adam and Eve disobeyed God, we read that when the Lord came and called to the man, he responded, saying, "I heard Your voice in the garden, and I was afraid because I was naked; and I hid myself" (Gen. 3:10). This account is a classic example of that first kind of fear of God, which results in an aversion to the object of that fear.

Questions along these lines are often raised: Is it right and desirable for a person to have this kind of dread with reference to God? Is this kind of fear any part of the fear of God that is commanded and commended in Holy Scripture? Is this sense of dread and terror any part of that virtue which is such a dominant theme in Holy Scripture? The answer, as John Murray has so beautifully and accurately stated, is that "it is the essence of impiety not to be afraid of God when there is reason to be afraid of God."[2] Once Adam sinned, suppose he had sauntered up to God when God called and said, "Hello, how art Thou today, God? Nice to see Thee again. Have a great day!" Such a response to God would have been the essence of impiety and hardness of heart and the manifestation of a seared conscience. For if Adam had any remaining sense of who God was, of the terribleness of sinning against Him, and of the certainty that God's threat would be fulfilled, anything less than this fear of dread and anguish would have

---

2. Murray, *Principles of Conduct*, 233.

been the grossest form of impiety and brazen religious and moral folly.

This kind of fear is right and proper in every situation where our condition leaves us exposed to the righteous judgments of God. Is it right to be afraid of God? Yes, if you have biblical grounds to be afraid of Him. Was it right for Adam to be afraid? Of course it was. He had sinned against God. He had willfully and wickedly disobeyed the explicit command of God who said with respect to the tree of the knowledge of good and evil, "You shall not eat" (Gen. 2:17). Now, as God draws near to him, Adam is gripped with this dread, which leads him to attempt to run from God. Scripture warrants this dread of God whenever the cause of that dread is present. A clear example of this reality is found in Psalm 119:20. Here the psalmist declares, "My flesh trembles for fear of You, and I am afraid of Your judgments." Commenting on this verse, Michael Wilcock states: "Let us not assume complacently that that 'merely means reverence.' Verse 20 is about the shudder of dread; 'for our God is a consuming fire.'"[3]

Notice how this aspect of fear is commanded and commended in Holy Scripture in Deuteronomy 17:13. The context is a warning that if a man disregards the directives of the appointed judges in Israel, he is to be put to death. God clearly states one of the reasons for this command in verse 13: "And all the people shall hear and fear, and no longer act presumptuously." Imagine that the people go out one

---

3. Michael Wilcock, *The Message of Psalms 73–150* (Downers Grove, Ill.: InterVarsity Press, 2001), 211.

day for their neighborhood meeting, and they find that one of their friends is missing. Someone asks what happened to him. Another answers that he flouted the laws of God and was indifferent to the judges enforcing those laws—so he was taken out and stoned the day before. When the first person asks what the offense was, they explain that it was something relatively insignificant in itself. But the initial offense was not the issue as much as the man's disregard for the institution of the law and the administration of that law by God's directive. So the man was put to death. His friends are filled with fear. There is a dread lest anyone else dare do as he did and get what he got. And God said that the very purpose for which He gave this directive was that His people might be possessed by the fear of God—a fear that has dread and terror in it.

In Deuteronomy 21, God directs the Israelites how to deal with a stubborn and rebellious son who, in spite of the faithful discipline of his parents, refuses to walk in the ways that they have commanded him. When the situation seems hopeless, these directives are given:

> Then his father and his mother shall take hold of him and bring him out to the elders of his city, to the gate of his city. And they shall say to the elders of his city, "This son of ours is stubborn and rebellious; he will not obey our voice; he is a glutton and a drunkard." Then all the men of his city shall stone him to death with stones; so you shall put away the evil from among you, and all Israel shall hear and fear (Deut. 21:19–21).

We could imagine an Israelite teenage boy who was tempted to be a smart aleck toward his parents. He begins to do what the "in thing" is in his particular tent neighborhood and starts mouthing off about his dad and mom and showing how smart-alecky he can be. Then one day his group gets together to have their clandestine session of bragging to one another about how they have been able to get away with things at home. On that day, one of their cohorts doesn't show up, and some of them begin to wonder where Isaac is. "Didn't you hear what happened to Isaac?" say the others. "No, what happened to him?" The answer to this question comes back—"His dad and mom took him to the elders. Now, he's dead under a pile of stones." Suddenly the air of gaiety leaves the little group, and they stop their bragging. The group gradually dissipates, and they go to their homes, gripped with dread and fear, lest by coming into the same sphere of guilt, the same condemnation come on them. God gives this mandate not only to put away evil so that it will not be infectious, but to put fear into the hearts of the people. This is the fear of dread, the fear of terror.

New Testament Witness

But someone says, "That is in the shadowy, right-angled, iron-clad climate of the Old Testament. The New Testament creates a new climate." Does it? Listen to the words of our Lord Jesus: "My friends, do not be afraid of those who kill the body, and after that have no more that they can do. But I will show you whom you should fear: Fear Him who, after He has killed, has power to cast into hell; yes, I say to you, fear Him!" (Luke 12:4–5).

What is this fear that Jesus commands? It is not the fear of veneration and awe. Rather, it is the fear of dread and terror. Jesus says that if you begin to contemplate conducting yourself in a way that warrants the damnation of God, you should be gripped with terrible dread. The God who condemns such conduct has power to cast into hell. Our Lord not only *commends* this kind of fear, He *commands* it.

A similar passage is found in Romans 11:20–21 where the apostle has written concerning the fact that natural Israel has come under the judgment of God because of its unbelief. He says that "because of unbelief they were broken off." He then goes on to say that since God broke off the natural branches because of their unbelief, then we Gentiles who have been grafted into God's redemptive privileges are under obligation not to "be haughty, but fear."

We find the writer to the Hebrews exhorting his readers, some of whom have begun to waver in their faith, to press on into the full knowledge of Christ and into an unswerving commitment to the Christian faith. Some of them who had been enlightened, who had tasted the good word of God and the powers of the world to come, were being tempted to repudiate their attachment to Christ and to the blessings of the new covenant and to go back to the old, shadowy forms and rituals of Judaism. He says in one of his exhortations, "Therefore, since a promise remains of entering His rest, let us fear lest any of you seem to have come short of it" (Heb. 4:1). What fear is that? It is the fear of horror and dread at the thought that they might fail to enter into full gospel rest in the way of persevering faith.

Failing to enter in, they would find themselves under the condemnation of God.

In chapter 10, the writer expands the same thought:

> For if we sin willfully after we have received the knowledge of the truth, there no longer remains a sacrifice for sins, but a certain fearful expectation of judgment, and fiery indignation which will devour the adversaries. Anyone who has rejected Moses' law dies without mercy on the testimony of two or three witnesses. Of how much worse punishment, do you suppose, will he be thought worthy who has trampled the Son of God underfoot, counted the blood of the covenant by which he was sanctified a common thing, and insulted the Spirit of grace? For we know Him who said, "Vengeance is Mine, I will repay," says the Lord. And again, "The LORD will judge His people." It is a fearful thing to fall into the hands of the living God (Heb. 10:26–31).

Do you hear what he is saying? He is saying that if a man repudiates Christ and the distinctive redemptive blessings found only in Him and thereby places himself in a position in which the judgment of God is inevitable, then he should be filled with fear as he expects that judgment to fall—for it is a fearful thing to fall into the hands of the living God. For a man to believe himself to be a candidate of the judgment of God *and not to fear* is to show a total insensitivity to all that Scripture reveals about the character of God and the terror of His judgment.

The Legitimacy of Feelings of Dread and
Terror toward God

Therefore, is it right to have this aspect of the fear of God, this dread or terror of the Lord? To that question the Scripture gives a clear yes. But a second question is, what lies at the root of this dread and fear? Negatively, it is not necessarily or exclusively a work of God's grace, for this fear is found in unconverted people. But positively, *that which lies at the root of this fear is some comprehension of the character of God as holy and just.* Because He is holy, He is passionately opposed to all sin. Because He is just, He must punish all sin. It is the recognition of who God is as a holy and just God and, consequently, how He regards sin that lies at the root of this fear of dread and terror. It is what Adam knew of the holy character of God, a holiness that had been stamped upon his own inner being but was now marred by his sin. It is what he knew of the character of God as holy and just that caused him to attempt to hide from God when he heard that voice calling to him. God's voice produced in Adam a fear of dread and terror.

As we read through the Scriptures, we find such phrases as "the fury of [God's] anger" (Isa. 42:25) and the pouring out of His "indignation" (Ezek. 21:31). We read such expressions as "indignation and wrath" (Rom. 2:8) and of our Lord Jesus coming in the company of "His mighty angels, in flaming fire taking vengeance on those who do not know God, and on those who do not obey the gospel of our Lord Jesus Christ" (2 Thess. 1:7–8). What do such expressions and statements communicate to us? It is the biblical concept that when omnipotence wields the sword of vengeance and the infinite God takes the finite creature into His hands for judgment, that such a creature ought to tremble with horror and dread—for it is indeed a "fearful thing to fall into the hands of the living God" (Heb. 10:31). And it is only ignorance of the character of God or spiritual insanity that would keep a man from this type of fear of God if he were in the path that leads to God's judgment. The Scriptures tell us that when that day of God's wrath actually arrives, men from all positions and stations in life will cry out to the rocks and the hills to fall on them and to hide them from "the face of Him who sits on the throne and from the wrath of the Lamb" (Rev. 6:16).

What would you think if you saw a man walking down a railroad track while a train three hundred yards away was bearing down on him at seventy miles per hour, yet the man just kept walking down the center of the track toward the oncoming train, whistling a familiar folk tune? You would conclude that one of two things was wrong with him: either he was blind and deaf and therefore utterly ignorant of what was about to overtake and completely destroy him; or, if he had eyes and ears and all his faculties of perception, he was insane. For whatever reason, he cannot relate the onrush of those tons of cold steel at that speed to what they will do to his body, to his life. He is a man either completely oblivious or insane who does not perceive nor react in an appropriate way to the facts that are obvious to everyone else. He is out of touch with reality. Hence, he has no fear. In the same way, the only reason any unconverted person does not find himself gripped with a constant terror and dread of God is that he is either spiritually blind or spiritually insane. He is blind to the character of the God of the Bible, or, having been made acquainted with that character, he is so filled with spiritual insanity that he can make no connection between the fury of God's wrath and his own certain reception of that wrath in judgment.

Are you reading these words as a stranger to the God of heaven and His salvation offered to sinners in Jesus Christ? If so, then you know that it is difficult to shove out of your mind this aspect of the dread and terror of God. No man likes to live in dread and terror. Every son of Adam, prior to a work of God's grace in his heart, tries to rid himself of that terror. What does he do? He tries to convince himself that the locomotive is only a papier-mâché plaything, and he attempts to tamper with the character of God. He will try to convince himself that God loves His creatures too much to inflict eternal destruction on them. Psalm 50 describes just such a man. In verses 16–20, Asaph describes a man who professes to be a true believer, but his lifestyle contradicts that profession. To such a one God says:

> These things you have done, and I kept silent;
> You thought that I was altogether like you;
> But I will rebuke you,
> And set them in order before your eyes.
>
> Now consider this, you who forget God,
> Lest I tear you in pieces,
> And there be none to deliver. (Ps. 50:21–22)

I once read some sermons preached by a minister in a liberal church on the subject of the future life. At one point he said, "Now, of one thing I am absolutely sure: God would never send one of His creatures to hell. That I know." One would expect a man to at least make an attempt to back up such a dogmatic assertion with some twisted verses. He did not produce one verse from Scripture to prove his claim! What was he doing? He was standing on the tracks, beholding the train coming, knowing it would destroy him, yet trying to convince himself that it's not a train made of tons of steel that would crush him. He tells himself—and, in his case, others—that it is simply a mirage. That is what lies behind all the attempts of men to change the character of God. As long as God is absolutely holy and inflexibly just, they know that these aspects of God's character will demand and inflict judgment and damnation on them. Such a thought makes them immeasurably uncomfortable.

Even the heathen who have never seen one page of the Bible experience something of this fear of terror and dread. We read about it in Romans 1:32: they know "the righteous judgment of God." We read in Romans 2:15 that their thoughts accuse them. Yet men continue to tell themselves that the train of judgment is not coming—no, it is just a mirage. They will either seek to deny the existence of those aspects of His character that demand judgment, or they will find some way to utterly blunt their senses in an attempt to remove these thoughts completely from their minds.

Let me further establish this crucial observation. No rational man or woman would deny that manifold benefits have been conferred on humanity by means of technology—those means by which sights, sounds, and images can be transmitted across continents at the speed of light. Christians should not question how these inventions and tools have advanced the spread of the gospel and the knowledge of the Word of God in our generation. In many cases, they have also made life more delightful (i.e., grandparents in California being able to Skype with their grandchildren in Alabama), enjoyable, comfortable, safe, productive, and efficient.

However, mere thoughtful observation of people around us buttressed by responsibly gathered data demonstrates that for multitudes of men, women, boys, and girls this technology has become nothing less than tragically addictive. I am prepared to assert that one of the major influences driving this kind of addiction is that of the god of this world who is seeking to inoculate people from serious thoughts about the God of inflexible justice and burning holiness whom they will soon meet in judgment. If indeed the fear of the Lord is the beginning of knowledge, what better way to shut men up in damning ignorance of that fear but to crowd out serious and reflective consideration of who God is.

What makes incessant television watching such a national pastime in our own country and in other places where people have easy access to TV and the host of other electronic and digital gadgets by which they continually fill their ears with sounds and their eyes with images of one kind or another? What produces the addictive patterns in the use of electronic devices such as iPods, Smartphones, and Internet social networking? I suggest that when all lesser issues are said to be the answer to why these patterns exist, the main reason behind them is this: People passionately desire to avoid facing the reality of God's judgment. Men

don't want to leave themselves alone with their thoughts *Pascal.*
for five minutes. Unless their consciences have been totally
seared, they fear the silence that augments the sound of the
rumbling of the wheels of an onrushing God, coming to
judge, and they see themselves on the tracks. They may say
that they do not believe in God. But they possess at least
some apprehension of the character of God as holy and just
and that they are on the way to judgment (see Rom. 1:32).
They reason, "If only I can so fill my mind with other things
between now and then, I won't have any agony until it over-
takes me." So they become obsessed with sounds and sights
and other forms of mind-absorbing banal activity.

The Legitimacy of Dread and Terror in the Child of God
The next question is, what about the child of God who
knows he is accepted in the beloved One, the person who
knows that the train of judgment for his sin has crushed
his Lord but will never crush him? Should such a child of
God, who knows that there is no condemnation for him
in Christ Jesus, experience any of this aspect of the fear of
God? Should he know any dread, any terror? Doesn't the
apostle John tell us that "there is no fear in love; but perfect love casts out fear, because fear involves torment. But he
who fears has not been made perfect in love" (1 John 4:18)?

This text is not intended to be a negation of the legitimacy of any fear of dread or terror in the heart of a true
child of God. Rather, it informs us that if we embrace
God's love to us in Jesus Christ, the overall ethos and climate of our relationship with God will not be marked by
a prevailing pattern of tormenting fear and dread of God.

However, this one text was never placed in the Scriptures in order to cancel many other texts and their clear teaching that there is still a limited place for the fear of dread and terror in the heart and life of a true child of God.

Even before Adam sinned, this element of the fear of God was intended to be part of what deterred him from sin. When God gave the command concerning the forbidden tree, He couched it in the form of a threat, one intended to produce in Adam a fear of God's certain punishment were he to disobey God. He said, "Of every tree of the garden you may freely eat; but of the tree of the knowledge of good and evil you shall not eat, for in the day that you eat of it you shall surely die" (Gen. 2:16–17). The Lord could have stopped at the point of having simply given the command; but to enforce the command and to give added motivation to obedience, what did He do? He made a threat. In effect, He said to Adam, "If you begin to think about eating of that tree, Adam, listen: In the day that you eat of it, you will surely die" (cf. v. 17). In essence, God was saying, "Adam, if you have any dread of Me as a God of judgment, don't eat, or you are going to put yourself on the train tracks of My judgment."

If God determined that fear of His judgment was to be a legitimate motive to Adam in his unfallen state, how much more is it a necessary motive for us who are in a redeemed state but not yet perfected and living out our days in the context of a world that continually appeals to various facets of our remaining corruption? The sin that is still within us and about us can have terrible, even frightening effects on us and bring great reproach to the name of our God and cause us to be wounded and pierced through in many ways by God's chastening hand. Furthermore, for all professing Christians, the danger of apostasy is real. It is not surprising then to find saints in both the Old and New Testaments confessing that they fear God's judgments.

Consider Psalm 119:120: "My flesh trembles for fear of You, and I am afraid of Your judgments." This is the type of trembling that the nine-year-old boy who sees the bully headed toward him experiences. This is not the trembling of awe—the psalmist mentions that in other places. But here he is contemplating God's being and attributes, and he trembles. He is contemplating what it would be like when this God whom he knows by divine revelation—this God whom he has come to see and love in all the magnitude and glory of His holiness and power—takes men in hand for judgment. Just the contemplation of it, he says, causes his flesh to tremble! The believer has a greater and more accurate view of the character of God than the unbeliever. And when he contemplates the more intimidating aspects of God's character as they relate to judgment, he cannot help but tremble because he knows God is true.

Once more I take up the common objection to this teaching that presents itself with the words, "That's the *Old* Testament." Does the New Testament present us with a different perspective? Not at all. In fact, the New Testament only enforces this perspective. We read in 1 Peter 1:17 this clear command of Scripture: "And if you call on the Father, who without partiality judges according to each one's work, conduct yourselves throughout the time of your stay here *in fear*" (emphasis added). Never permit yourself to become <u>irresponsibly giddy and so flippantly</u> <u>overconfident</u> that you forget you are dealing with a God who judges without respect of persons. Let there be something of holy dread (but not of crippling dread) about you throughout the entirety of your days. This crippling dread is often manifested in those believers who are so fearful of presumption and self-deception that they never come to a settled confidence of their acceptance in Christ. This kind of crippling dread neither glorifies God nor does justice to the promises of the gospel.

Should the child of God be characterized in any way by this fear of dread? Yes, he should. The fear of dread is not to be the dominant element of the fear of God in the Christian, but it is nonetheless a vital part of what comprises the fear of the Lord, which is the chief part of wisdom (see Heb. 4:1).

The Crucial Nature of This Dread and Terror

As you ponder this subject, are you doing so as a stranger to vital union with Christ and to the regenerating work of the Holy Spirit? Do you bear any marks of a saving union with Christ and of a true disciple? If so, have you no dread of God's awful judgment? In Psalm 90:11, Moses asks the question, "Who knows the power of Your anger? For as the fear of You, so is Your wrath." Do you believe that God is the God He has revealed Himself to be in Scripture? If He is such a God, then His judgments are bearing down on you just like the train bearing down on that man on the railroad tracks. Can you contemplate that reality without any inward trembling and dread? Can you consider the onrushing judgment of God and remain a stranger to grace and to the cleansing of the blood of Christ, which alone can save you from that judgment? Do you resent the thought that someone would attempt to scare you into becoming a Christian? Suppose someone were to yell to that man on the tracks, "Man, a train is coming. Get off the tracks!" Would he not be trying to scare him out of the way of impending danger and disaster? Indeed, he would be! But he would not be scaring him with a phantom terror. He would be scaring him with naked realities, the reality of hardened steel that will crush that man's throbbing flesh unless he gets off the tracks.

When you hear the warning, "Flee from the wrath to come!," you ought to repent! Give yourself no rest until you know that you are joined to Christ. The time between now and the day of judgment will be but a few short seconds as God reckons time. Should you die an untimely death, that day will come even more swiftly for you. May God grant that you will fear with a fear that will cause you to flee from your sin and from His wrath and judgment. This was the burden of John the Baptist when he said to those of his generation, "Who warned you to flee from the wrath to come?" (Matt. 3:7).

And for the people of God, let us not be caught up in the notion that the essence of spirituality is the measure to which we can carelessly disregard the judgments of the Almighty God and the terror of the Lord. As one has said, humility, contrition, and lowliness of mind are the essence of biblical godliness. The dispositional complex that is characterized by these fruits of the Spirit must embrace the fear and trembling that reflect our consciousness of our sin and frailty. The piety of the New Testament is totally alien to the presumption of the person who is a stranger to a contrite heart. And it is alien to the confidence of the person who never takes account of the holy and just judgments of God. A wholesome, holy dread is no small part of our motivation to persevere in the faith. When sin becomes so seductive and attractive in its overtures, and it seems as though the reality of a dying Savior and all the other motives of grace have suddenly been smothered in our minds and hearts, this is one motive that God often uses to awaken His children. The familiar warning, "The wages of sin is death" (Rom. 6:23), was written to *believers*—the saints in the church at Rome. Writing to the same believers at Rome, the apostle Paul urges these believers to continually mortify their sin by warning them with the words, "For if you live according to the flesh you will die" (Rom. 8:13).

Finally, this fear should motivate us not only with reference to ourselves, but with respect to our concern for others. The apostle Paul wrote in 2 Corinthians 5:10–11, "For we must all appear before the judgment seat of Christ, that each one may receive the things done in the body, according to what he has done, whether good or bad. Knowing, therefore, the terror of the Lord, we persuade men; but we are well known to God, and I also trust are well known in your consciences." If you see the train bearing down on another man, you don't stand there and whistle and say, "Well, at least it's not going to hit *me*." Just the thought of what the train will do to him will make you tremble and do everything you can to persuade the man to get off the tracks. Likewise, the child of God who has been rescued from the onrushing locomotive and knows from what he has been delivered cannot help but tremble as he beholds the train of God's fury and wrath bearing down on others. Thus, the terror of the Lord becomes part of the motivation to persuade men to flee the wrath to come. We are instructed by Jude with these words: "And on some have compassion, making a distinction; but others save *with fear,* pulling them out of the fire, hating even the garment defiled by the flesh" (Jude 22–23, emphasis added).

May God grant that this aspect of His fear will become an increasing part of our hearts and minds. May it have its commensurate effect in our lives. The presence of this dread and terror is no sure evidence of grace. You may, like Felix, tremble and still be impenitent (Acts 24:25). But it is doubtful there is any saving grace where this fear is not present, for grace has introduced you to the knowledge of God, the God who is terrible in His judgment.

Before leaving our consideration of this fear of dread, I urge the reader to give careful attention to these words of John Calvin:

> For, to begin with, the pious mind does not dream up for itself any God it pleases, but contemplates the one and only true God. And it does not attach to him whatever it pleases, but is content to hold him to be as he manifests himself; furthermore the mind always exercises the utmost diligence and care not to wander astray, or rashly or boldly to go beyond his will.... *Because it sees him to be a righteous judge, armed with severity to punish wickedness, it ever holds his*

judgment seat before its gaze, and through fear *of him restrains itself from provoking his anger.* Besides, this mind restrains itself from sinning, not out of dread of punishment alone; but, because it loves and reveres God as Father, it worships and adores him as Lord.[4]

The Fear of Veneration and Awe

Without negating or diluting that first facet of the fear of God—the fear of terror and dread—nevertheless, it is the second aspect of the fear of God that is the dominant theme of Holy Scripture with respect to believers. When Scripture says, "The fear of the LORD is the beginning of knowledge," it is not so much the fear of terror and of dread that is in view, but the fear of veneration, awe, and reverence. It is primarily this fear God says He will put into the hearts of men in the blessings of the new covenant that will cause them to adhere to His ways and to keep His statutes (Jer. 32:39–41).

Old Testament Examples

What must there be in a man if he is to have *this* fear of God, the fear of awe and reverence? We may think through this second aspect of the fear of God by considering some biblical examples of it. We can start by looking at some Old Testament examples.

Jacob. In Genesis 28:12–22, we have the account of Jacob's dream. In his dream, he sees a ladder and angels ascending

---

4. John Calvin, *Institutes of the Christian Religion* (Philadelphia: Westminster John Knox Press, 1967), 42–43. Emphasis added.

and descending on it. In the midst of this very strange vision, he hears the voice of Jehovah, the God of the covenant, who comes to renew that covenant with him. When he woke from his dream and began to reflect on it, he came to certain conclusions.

His first conclusion is stated very clearly in verse 16: "Surely the LORD is in this place, and I did not know it." He says, in essence, "I came out and camped under the open skies, and I had no thought of the immediate presence of God, but I was mistaken. The Lord Himself is in this place, and I was unaware of it." Jacob then consciously reflects on the fact that the Lord Jehovah, the great God of creation, the great God of covenant-making and covenant-keeping promise, had indeed been there, and that he had actually been in His presence. Then the reflex action of Jacob's whole being is this: "And he was afraid and said, 'How awesome is this place! This is none other than the house of God, and this is the gate of heaven!'" (v. 17). That is, "If God is here, and if He is the God He declared Himself to be in my vision—the God of Abraham and Isaac, the God of creation, the great God of my fathers—and if I am what I know myself to be—Jacob, a fallen son of Adam, a weak creature of the dust—that I should be in the presence of this great God! How awesome is this place! This is none other than the house of God, and this is the gate of heaven."

Is this fear that Jacob exhibits a fear of terror and anguish that makes him want to run? No, for the subsequent paragraph indicates that it was a fear that was coupled with the tenderest characteristics of trust in the faithfulness of God and of confidence in the love and mercy of God. It was a fear that is perfectly consistent with trust and love. This we see when he then raises a pillar and says it will be a monument to the faithfulness of this same God whose presence is dreadful, but who will nonetheless care for him, fulfill His promise, and bring him again to this place. And out of gratitude to God, Jacob vows to give to this truly awesome and gracious God the tenth of all that he possesses.

This is a beautiful and clear example of this second aspect of the fear of God. Though it says that Jacob was afraid, and though he even uses the term "awesome," his was not that fear of dread and terror that makes a man want to run from the object feared, like the little boy who runs from a bully. It is a dread and a fear that is perfectly consistent with a desire to be in the presence of the object of that fear and to render to that object honor and worship, love and obedience.

Moses. Another illustration is from Exodus 3:1–6:

> Now Moses was tending the flock of Jethro his father-in-law, the priest of Midian. And he led the flock to the back of the desert, and came to Horeb, the mountain of God. And the Angel of the LORD appeared to him in a flame of fire from the midst of a bush. So he looked, and behold, the bush was burning with fire, but the bush was not consumed. Then Moses said, "I will now turn aside and see this great sight, why the bush does not burn." So when the LORD saw that he turned aside to look, God called to him from the midst of the bush and said, "Moses, Moses!" And he said, "Here I am." Then He said, "Do not draw near this place. Take your sandals off your feet, for the place

where you stand is holy ground." Moreover He said, "I am the God of your father—the God of Abraham, the God of Isaac, and the God of Jacob." And Moses hid his face, for he was afraid to look upon God.

Here is Moses, out tending sheep. Suddenly, he notices a bush that has burst into flames. He wants to figure out why the bush is burning but not consumed. That is the only reason Scripture gives as to why he turns aside. An unnatural phenomenon caught his eye, and he is curious. But God says, "Moses, don't even think of coming near just to do a little scientific investigation. I, the God of Abraham, Isaac, and Jacob, have a word to say to you." And when Moses recognized that God was there, we are told that, instead of going over and analyzing the bush, "Moses hid his face, for he was afraid to look upon God" (v. 6).

Here is a clear statement that Moses was filled with a fear of God. But was it a fear that made him want to run from God? No, for that same God then reveals His compassion for His people and His purpose to deliver them (vv. 7–8). And rather than run from Him, as Adam did, Moses drew near with true reverence to commune with God and talk with Him face to face. So the fear of God that caused Moses to hide his face is not the least bit inconsistent with the most intimate dealings with God. Moses hides his face, yet he talks with God. It is a fear of reverential awe, veneration, and honor.

Isaiah. The last example for us to consider in the Old Testament is Isaiah 6:1–5, another familiar passage:

> In the year that King Uzziah died, I saw the Lord sitting on a throne, high and lifted up, and the train of His robe filled the temple. Above it stood seraphim; each one had six wings: with two he covered his face, with two he covered his feet, and with two he flew. And one cried to another and said: "Holy, holy, holy is the LORD of hosts; The whole earth is full of His glory!" And the posts of the door were shaken by the voice of him who cried out, and the house was filled with smoke. So I said: "Woe is me, for I am undone! Because I am a man of unclean lips, and I dwell in the midst of a people of unclean lips; for my eyes have seen the King, the LORD of hosts."

Both the prophet and the celestial hosts looked on the same object. What is the reaction of the seraphim as they behold this sight of God? They are filled with a holy restlessness. They cannot, as it were, pause and fix their position before the throne, but it says they fly about the throne. Further, they cover their feet and faces. They are some form of angelic beings who have never known sin, yet in the presence of that great God, they veil their faces and feet. As Moses hid his face and said, "I am afraid to look on God," so they hide their faces and cover their feet, overcome, filled with awe at the holiness of God. And they cry one to another, "Holy, holy, holy is the LORD of hosts; the whole earth is full of His glory!"

Of course, there is no indication of any sense of grief or self-effacing shame because of sin on the part of the seraphim. But that is not the case when the prophet looks on this same God; for when he beholds the same object the seraphim saw, he is not only overcome by the immensity and the transcendent majesty of God in His holiness, but there is an added dimension of response. There is a reflexive reaction of grief, self-effacing shame, conviction, and contrition. This is not just a creature like the seraphim, looking on the exalted Creator; this is a sinful creature looking on the thrice-holy God. Therefore, the only fitting reaction is a fear of reverential awe that is mingled with the sense of uncleanness, which in turn produces conviction and contrition.

This is the only disposition fitting for a sinful creature who gazes on a holy God. Seraphim may veil their faces and cry, "Holy, holy, holy," with no shame of sin. But you and I can't. And if it is incongruous and out of place for sinless beings like seraphim to be in the presence of God without this reverential awe, how much more is it out of place for sinful men and women, laden with iniquity, to draw near to His presence without that reverence and godly fear coupled with a deep sense of self-effacing shame because of our sin?

Then God imparts to his shattered servant the symbols and words of pardoning and cleansing grace. Isaiah 6:6–7 reads, "Then one of the seraphim flew to me, having in his hand a live coal which he had taken with the tongs from the altar. And he touched my mouth with it, and said: 'Behold, this has touched your lips; your iniquity is taken away, and your sin purged.'"

However, this shattering vision of God in His holiness and His flesh-withering transcendence did not cause the prophet to run from God. Rather, having been assured of God's cleansing and forgiveness, Isaiah overhears an intratrinitarian conversation concerning who will go to the nation of Israel as God's messenger. Hearing that conversation, the forgiven and cleansed prophet draws near to this God and offers himself for that task. The fear of God that shattered him, now overlaid and suffused with the awareness of divine forgiveness and cleansing, was also the fear that captured his affections and will and brought him in loving submission to the call of God.

New Testament Example

Someone may once again object that this is the climate of the *Old* Testament. In the Lord Jesus, they may say, there has come an overshadowing revelation of the softer lines of God's character. Is that true? One account in the Gospels will forever abolish such a thought. In Luke, we have an incident in the life of Jesus who came for the express purpose of revealing the Father—as He said, "He who has seen Me has seen the Father" (John 14:9). "No one has seen God at any time. The only begotten Son, who is in the bosom of the Father, He has declared Him" (John 1:18). The incident to which I make reference is a familiar one in which Peter and his friends have been fishing all night and have caught nothing. Jesus has just used Peter's boat as a kind of pulpit from which to teach the people on the shore. When our Lord was done teaching the people, He said to Peter:

> "Launch out into the deep and let down your nets for a catch." But Simon answered and said to Him, "Master, we have toiled all night and caught nothing; nevertheless at Your word I will let down the net." And when they had done this, they caught a great number of fish, and their net was breaking. So they signaled to their partners in the other boat to come

and help them. And they came and filled both the boats, so that they began to sink. When Simon Peter saw it, he fell down at Jesus' knees, saying, "Depart from me, for I am a sinful man, O Lord!" For he and all who were with him were astonished at the catch of fish which they had taken; and so also were James and John, the sons of Zebedee, who were partners with Simon. And Jesus said to Simon, "Do not be afraid. From now on you will catch men." So when they had brought their boats to land, they forsook all and followed Him (Luke 5:4–11).

How can we bring these two apparently contradictory reactions together? On the one hand, Peter tells the Lord to depart from him because he is a sinful man, yet he forsakes all and follows Jesus Christ. What had happened to Peter? Peter got the message of this act of our Lord. He saw behind the fact that the net was put down and a great multitude of fish was enclosed. He recognized—to what degree at this point we do not know—that the one who did this could be none other than the Son of God, the Messiah. When that recognition dawned on him, his reaction was to fall at Jesus' feet, overcome with a sense of reverential awe and dread that made him blurt out, "Depart from me, Lord. It is not fit that I, a sinful man, should be in such close proximity to the Lord of creation!" Yet that very reaction was coupled with the most intense longing to be with Him—so much so that Peter leaves his business, home, and friends and follows Christ.

There is no clashing of spiritual experience here. Without these two aspects of spiritual experience being present in the heart of a man, it is doubtful if there is any true attachment to the Christ of the Scriptures. It is a faulty notion that we can just snuggle up to Jesus and feel so much at home with Him without any sense of our sinfulness making us want to cry out, "Depart from me, Lord. It is not fit that we should enter into an intimate relationship." And yet, wonder of wonders, Christ so reveals to us the heart of God in its love and forgiveness that we cling to Him. And, like these disciples, we are, by His grace, willing to forsake all to follow Him.

It is a repetition, in a sense, of Isaiah 6. Here is not only a creature in the presence of deity, but also a *sinful* creature who senses that something is wrong that he should be so close to this holy God. "Depart from me, Lord." And yet at the same time, when the commission comes, there is the glad response, even as there was with Isaiah. There is a fear, unlike that fear of dread and terror, that makes a person want to run from its object. This fear, this awe, this reverential veneration is perfectly consistent with the intimate attachment of faith and love to the object of that fear.

Summary

To summarize, I believe it is accurate to say that *the fear of God, which is the soul of godliness, is a fear that consists in awe, reverence, and honor, and all of these things in a profound measure of their exercise.* It is the reaction of our minds and souls to a sight of God in His majesty and holiness. As John Murray has so accurately said in seeking to define the fear of God, "The controlling sense of the majesty and holiness of God and the profound reverence which this apprehension draws forth constitute the essence of the fear of God."[5] John Brown gives this definition of the fear of God in his exposition of 1 Peter 2:17:

> We are to *fear* him: that is, we are to cherish an awful [reverential] sense of his infinite grandeur and excellence, corresponding to the revelation he has made of these things in His Word and in His works, inducing in us a conviction that his favor is the greatest of all blessings, and his disapprobation [disapproval] the greatest of all evils, and manifesting itself in leading us practically to seek his favor as the chief good we can enjoy, and to avoid his disapprobation as the most tremendous evil we can be subjected to. Such is the fear which the Christian man ought to cherish and manifest towards God.[6]

The practical influence of the fear of God is clearly seen when the apostle Paul, describing the state of all men by nature, gives a pivotal and capstone description of the state of unconverted men in Romans 3:18: "There is no fear of God before their eyes." Do you, dear reader, live a life of utter indifference to the claims of God's holy law and to the overtures of the gospel of His dear Son? Do you know why you live that way? It is because you do not live life with the fear of God before your eyes. You look at life as nothing more than one extended opportunity to pursue what will please you. What your lusts dictate, you do. What your

---

5. Murray, *Principles of Conduct*, 237.

6. John Brown, *Expository Discourses on First Peter* (Evansville, Ind.: The Sovereign Grace Book Club, 1958), 2:115.

desires and appetites crave, you pursue. The fear of God—that controlling sense of His majesty and holiness and the profound reverence that it draws forth—is nothing to you. No part of it dwells in you. If that is the case with you, my friend, may God by His Spirit teach you the fear of the Lord before it is too late (Ps. 34:11; Prov. 2:1–5).

Questions for Reflection and Discussion

1. What is significant about the use of the word "fear" in its general biblical usage?

2. What are the two fundamental kinds of fear taught and illustrated in the Scriptures?

3. Where in the Scriptures is the fear of dread and terror first encountered, and was this fear legitimate? If so, why?

4. Should this fear of dread and terror have any place in the life and Christian experience of the true child of God? If so, when?

5. What are some of the most prominent examples of the fear of veneration and awe recorded in the Old Testament? The New Testament?

───── ◆ ─────

CHAPTER THREE

Ingredients of the Fear of God

In the previous two chapters, we have seen the pervasive presence of this central theme in Scripture and attempted to illustrate and define the fear of God from the Bible. We will now apply ourselves to discovering the essential ingredients of the fear of God. We will identify the three categories of biblical truth that constitute the essential ingredients of the fear of God. First, we must have correct concepts of the character of God. Second, we must have a widespread sense of the presence of God. Third, we must have a constant awareness of our obligations to God.

Correct Concepts of the Character of God

God Is Majestic in Holiness

Although we considered the following passage earlier, we turn to it again under the heading of our present concern. Revelation 15:4 asks a question: "Who shall not fear You, O Lord, and glorify Your name?" Here are the victorious saints—the redeemed who have overcome the beast and his image. They are in the presence of God, and we read, in verses 2–4:

> And I saw something like a sea of glass mingled with fire, and those who have the victory over the beast, over his image and over his mark and over the number of his name, standing on the sea of glass, having harps of God. They sing the song of Moses, the servant of God, and the song of the Lamb, saying:
>
> "Great and marvelous are Your works,
> Lord God Almighty!
> Just and true are Your ways,
> O King of the saints!
> Who shall not fear You, O Lord, and glorify Your name?
> For You alone are holy.
> For all nations shall come and worship before You,
> for Your judgments have been manifested."

As they behold their God, they praise Him. As they see Him for who He is and have right views of His character, ways, and judgments they ask, rhetorically, who shall not fear Him? They say, in essence, that anyone who sees God as they see Him must fear Him. This implies that correct concepts of the character of God are an indispensable element in producing the fear of God.

One of the great problems in our day is that we have in great measure lost sight of those aspects of the character of God that are calculated to produce His fear—namely, His majesty, immensity, holiness, and unrivaled sovereignty as the reigning monarch of the universe. Let me seek to illustrate this truth. It is as though we are looking at a landscape.

In the foreground there is a beautiful meadow, covered with swaying grasses and festooned with various wildflowers—the perfect picture of tranquility and peacefulness. But the backdrop of that landscape is composed of massive mountains with rugged, snow-capped peaks. Off to the sides and behind and above those mountains are great thunderhead clouds with lightning flashing and playing off the edges of the clouds. If a person focuses his attention only on the foreground of the scene, he may have a very accurate view of one part of it, but his response is inadequate with respect to the totality of that picture. If he can look at the scene and feel nothing but tranquility and ease and have no sense of awe and breathless wonder, it is because he is looking only at the foreground and not looking at the background as well. If you have ever been in the Rocky Mountains, you know what I mean. One receives a profound sense of being overpowered and swallowed up by the might, grandeur, majesty, and sheer massiveness of those mountains.

So it is with the character of God. The Scripture sets before us the softer hues of God's boundless mercy, unfathomable love and compassion, and fatherly tenderness. But never do the Scriptures set those attributes before us in isolation from the more intimidating and breathtaking characteristics of His holiness, wrath, immensity, eternity, omniscience, and omnipotence. In our day, many have lost sight of these aspects of the character of God. Therefore, we have greatly lost the experience of the fear of God.

The Cross Intensifies Our View of God's Holiness

Many tend to think that since God has revealed His love in the cross of Jesus Christ, it only remains for us to be enthralled with that love rather than to tremble in fear. But if, as Scripture tells us, sinless creatures hide their faces in the presence of the God of burning holiness (Isa. 6:1–3), why should we ever think that the sight of the wounds and the sacrifice of Christ will negate the necessity for us to draw near with veiled faces and with trembling hearts? It is accurate to say that perhaps nowhere in all of Scripture is this principle more clearly seen than in the cross itself—for what is the cross, if it is not God's clearest revelation of His inflexible justice and burning wrath as well as His amazing love and grace? What a display of inflexible justice it is when God spares not His own Son but brings on Him the full brunt of His wrath against sin! What a display of spotless holiness! God is so holy that He will turn His back on His only begotten, the one of whom He said, "This is My beloved Son, in whom I am well pleased" (Matt. 3:17). An enlightened view of the cross of Christ, rather than negating or diluting any part of the biblical teaching on the fear of God, serves to heighten and seal that disposition of heart so that all of our relationship to God through Christ is a relationship in the climate of the fear of God. Nowhere are we more inclined to obey the divine mandate to "serve the LORD with fear, and rejoice with trembling" (Ps. 2:11) than when we stand before an immolated God and receive the pardon purchased at the price of His blood.

To my unconverted friend, there will not be any measure of the fear of God in your heart until you begin to take seriously the revelation He has made of His own character and begin to tremble before Him with the fear of dread and terror—until you would cry for rocks and mountains to hide you from His face. And, dear friend, the gospel will then become good news to you—the good news that One experienced the hidden face of His Father so that you and I might be forgiven. That one is the Lord Jesus Christ.

If you are a child of God, you must be convinced that you will not grow in the fear of God unless you grow in your awareness of and sensitivity to the scriptural teaching concerning the immensity, majesty, and holiness of God. This is not something that is incorporated into our lives in a once-for-all spiritual experience. I would be intensely practical and exhort you to spend much time meditating on such portions of the Word of God as Isaiah 6 and 40 and Revelation 1 and 19 and some of the other passages that especially set forth God in His transcendent majesty, holiness, and immensity. Meditate on them until you begin to feel something of the climate of the biblical patterns of thought and take your place before Him in true godly fear.

It is this profound sense of His majesty and holiness that becomes one of the great motivations for a life of holiness and godliness. The first essential ingredient of the fear of God is a correct concept of God's character. If your thoughts of God have been such as to leave you devoid of His fear, there is something wrong with what you are thinking about God. May God help you to begin to conform your thinking to the statements of the Bible, that you might have that fear of the Lord which is the chief part of knowledge.

Once again, consider the words of John Murray relative to this point. "The fear of God in us is that frame of heart and mind which reflects our apprehension of who and what God is, and who and what God is will tolerate nothing less than totality of commitment to him."[1]

A Pervasive Sense of the Presence of God

Having demonstrated that the first element of the fear of God is correct concepts of the character of God, we now take up our consideration of the next element in the fear of God—a pervasive sense of His presence. It is a sense of the presence of God that spreads throughout the entirety of our lives so that there is no place or circumstance in which we find ourselves, but that we are conscious that God is here with us. He is here in all His majesty, holiness, fatherly love and compassion, and immensity—He is not "somewhere out there," but He is right here. The fear of God will always be constituted of this pervasive sense of the presence of God. It is for this reason that our fear of God will be perfected in heaven when we will experience the blessed reality of an unbroken and undiminished awareness of the immediate presence of God. This reality is captured in Revelation 21:3, "And I heard a loud voice from heaven saying, 'Behold, the tabernacle of God is with men, and He will dwell with them, and they shall be His people. God Himself will be with them and be their God.'"

---

1. Murray, *Principles of Conduct*, 242.

I remember years ago hearing a statement by the late Dr. A. W. Tozer. Insofar as my memory of his words is accurate, he said, "The most profound word in the human language is 'God.'" You can go to your dictionary to look up a word like "pervasive," as I did, and it says, "That which is spread throughout." You can define the word "pervasive." But try to define "God." Think of all the thousands of theological books that have been written in all the hundreds of languages throughout the earth trying to define God. If you could put them all together into one language and read them all, when you were all done you would have to say that you know only the edges of His being and His ways. The most profound word in the human language is "God." Then, as I remember, Tozer went on to say, "The most profound fact in all of human knowledge is the sentence, 'God is.'" All that the Scripture tells us about Him, He always has been and continues to be right now. God is not the great "I was," or the great "I shall be." Rather, He is the great and glorious "I am." And then the third thing Tozer said was this: "The most profound experience we can have consists in the recognition that 'God is *here*.'"

It is interesting to note that in many of the most notable instances where the fear of God is described for us in Scripture, it is described in a context of the realized presence of God. Think about some of the texts we have considered thus far in this study of the fear of God. "Then Jacob awoke from his sleep and said, 'Surely the LORD is in this place, and I did not know it'" (Gen. 28:16). We are told that Moses, at the burning bush, "was afraid to look upon God" (Ex. 3:6). Isaiah, when he beheld the Lord in a vision, said, "Woe is me, for I am undone!… For my eyes have seen the King, the LORD of hosts" (Isa. 6:5). If you trace out these examples of men who experienced the fear of God, you will find that very frequently they are set in a context where men are experiencing the manifested or realized presence of God. God is there, and they know He is there. They know that they are in His presence—a realization that moved them to the fear of God. Let us look more closely at several of these examples.

Psalm 139

There is a passage of Scripture that teaches this truth in a sustained and concentrated way. Psalm 139 describes, probably more clearly than any other text, a man who has right concepts of the character of God and who is at the same time convinced that this God, in His immensity, majesty, holiness, grace, and kindness, is right here. This man, David, is filled with a pervasive sense of the presence of God. He begins by expressing his consciousness of the omniscience of God—that is, the fact that this God knows all things:

> O LORD, You have searched me and known me.
> You know my sitting down and my rising up;
> You understand my thought afar off.
> You comprehend my path and my lying down,
> And are acquainted with all my ways.
> For there is not a word on my tongue, but behold,
>   O LORD, You know it altogether. (vv. 1–4)

Up to this point, David is describing what he knows about the character of God as an all-seeing, all-knowing God. But how is he looking at it? Is he looking at God's omniscience as if God were something like a spy satellite that can take pictures from many miles above the surface of the earth, yet produce photos that reveal the most minute of details? Is He this great, immense, all-knowing, all-seeing God who is up there, out there, somewhere, who sees and knows everything I do, like the great eye of the orbiting spy satellite? No—notice the transition in verse 5: "You have hedged me behind and before, and laid Your hand upon me." David is saying that the God who has searched and known him—who understands his thought and knows his every word—knows and understands *not* like the orbiting spy satellite, from miles and miles away, but He knows and understands him because His hand is on him. Notice how David goes on to develop this thought:

> Such knowledge is too wonderful for me;
> It is high, I cannot attain it.
> Where can I go from Your Spirit?
> Or where can I flee from Your presence?
> If I ascend into heaven, You are there;
> If I make my bed in hell, behold, You are there.
> (vv. 6–8)

David does not simply assert that he is unable to flee from God's *knowledge* or *omniscience*—he says he is not able to get away from His *presence*. He says that no matter how far he could travel in either direction—whether up into heaven itself or down to the grave, to Sheol—God would be there. God is not just *aware* of David; He is *there*. It is not just that He will *see* David; He will be there with him. In verses 9 and 10, David says,

If I take the wings of the morning,
And dwell in the uttermost parts of the sea,
Even there Your hand shall lead me,
And Your right hand shall hold me.

"The wings of the morning" is most likely a reference to the first rays of the sun as they break over the horizon and with the speed of light flash out over the Mediterranean Sea.

David obviously is not thinking in terms of "bare omniscience"—that God simply happens to know everything. Nor is he possessed with the notion that God is some heartless, formless being without personality who simply happens to be everywhere. Rather, he says, "Wherever I go, God is there, as the personal God whose hand is on me, whose hand holds me, whose hand covers me." He even traces this reality all the way back to his very conception in his mother's womb, into his subsequent prenatal development: "You formed my inward parts; You covered me in my mother's womb" (v. 13). Therefore, the fear of God to David consisted also of this second element, a pervasive sense of the presence of God. It is this sense that will create that awe, that sense of wonder, that sense of reverence which will make even the thought of disobeying such a God, of grieving Him by walking contrary to His will, unthinkable to a Christian. That is why Scripture says that the fear of the Lord is to depart from evil. If I am living in the sense of the immediate presence of this great God, I will be reluctant to defy the directives of His holy commandments and laws and offend Him to His face!

The Effect of Sensing God's Presence

How often have we been tempted to do something sinful, when the sudden appearance of another person has kept us from that sin? A child may be considering taking something that is forbidden to him—until his brother or sister walks into the room. If the presence of another creature, who has no power to judge him for his actions, has the effect of radically changing the child's conduct, what happens to the person who knows he is always in the immediate presence of the one before whom he is accountable for all that he does? Will it have any ethical and moral effect? Indeed, it will.

Suppose you lived on the East Coast of the United States. Something triggered in you a deep longing to visit the Grand Canyon. Suddenly, you had a passionate desire to find out all the facts concerning the Grand Canyon. You have never been there, but you want to learn all you can concerning this remarkable and majestic piece of God's creation. You begin to gather all the facts you can concerning the immensity, majesty, beauty, and transcendent splendor of the Grand Canyon. Further, you garner a good collection of the best books of photography that seek to capture its grandeur. Suppose you go further and memorize all those facts and even become an expert on the physical properties of the Grand Canyon. After several weeks of gathering all of this information and visual exposure to photos of the Grand Canyon, you ask yourself what difference all of this has made in your life. You then face the inescapable fact that all you have learned about the Grand Canyon has had very little, if any, influence on the way you think and live.

But suppose one morning you suddenly found yourself saddled on the back of a ray of light that broke over the eastern coast of the United States, and, with the snap of a finger, you stood right in the midst of the Grand Canyon. What would happen? You certainly wouldn't take out your tube of toothpaste and start brushing your teeth! Rather, you would say, "Amazing! Astonishing! Breathtaking! This is the Grand Canyon! Over the course of weeks I learned all these facts and figures about it, but this is the real thing! This is the Grand Canyon!" What has happened? Not one of all the facts and figures has changed. You can look out and see the mile or two-mile expanse. You can see the depth. You can see all the features you learned about. But what has happened? You have been put into the presence of the canyon itself. And all the characteristics of the Grand Canyon that you read about suddenly grip you with a sense of awe and wonder. Why? Because it is right there, and you are right in the middle of it.

That is what I am saying about God. You can have all the facts about God—good, biblical, and Reformed truths about God. He is holy, sovereign, transcendent, immense, free, boundless, and all the rest. But unless you learn to cultivate that all-pervasive sense of His presence, it won't make much difference in how you live. That's why some people, who may have a "smaller God" in terms of their theological understanding but still experience more of the sense of the presence of God, may live more godly and Christlike lives than others who have a "great big God" in their theology, but who have a distant God in their experience.

God is not the orbiting spy satellite. He is the ever-present, personal God. And in a certain sense, He is the very environment in which we live. As Paul said, "In him we live, and move, and have our being" (Acts 17:28). This is not pantheism. But it is a biblical concept that I fear that we know too little about experientially. Yet, this sense of the presence of God is an essential ingredient of the fear of God.

God's Presence with Abraham

Let us consider two illustrations of how this pervasive sense of God's presence has its practical effect upon the life of the man who experiences it. In Genesis 17:1, we read, "When Abram was ninety-nine years old, the LORD appeared to Abram and said to him, 'I am Almighty God; walk before Me and be blameless'"—that is, "Walk in the constant aware-ness of My eye on you, My presence with you, and your relationship to Me being the most important reality to you in every circumstance." And in the context of such a walk, "Be blameless." Here is the moral and ethical implication for a man who believes what is revealed about the character of God and cultivates an all-pervasive sense of the presence of God: He will live a life of obedience to that God. And this is exactly what we see in Genesis 22, when God commanded Abraham to take Isaac, the son of promise, and to offer him up as a burnt sacrifice. Just as Abraham is about to do the very thing that God told him, God prevents him from car-rying out the act. Notice what God says to him in verse 12: "*Now I know that you fear God*, since you have not withheld your son, your only son, from Me" (emphasis added). It was

Abraham's fear of God, rooted in his walking before God, that constrained him to this act of heroic obedience to God in being willing to sacrifice his beloved son Isaac.

God's Presence with Joseph

There is another striking example of this principle found in Genesis 39. Joseph is a handsome young man in Pharaoh's court, most likely constantly beholding the pervasive immorality characteristic of pagan religions. We have every reason to believe that he was a normal young man with normal heterosexual appetites and desires. Through no fault of his, he begins to receive sexual overtures from the wife of his boss, Potiphar. Joseph rejects her initial overtures. But she persists in her efforts to seduce him. One day, in absolute frustration, seeing that everyone else was out of the house, she actually laid hold of Joseph physically, begging him to engage in illicit intercourse with her. However, by the grace of God, Joseph resisted all of her wicked overtures and ran away from her, leaving his coat clutched in her hands. This frustrated "lady of the night" uses Joseph's coat as collaborating evidence to "prove" that he had made immoral advances to her. This resulted in Joseph being thrown in prison.

However, in the midst of this intense period of temptation, Joseph reveals what it was that preserved him through this trial. He says to Potiphar's wife in Genesis 39:9, speaking of his master Potiphar, "There is no one greater in this house than I, nor has he kept back anything from me but you, because you are his wife. How then can I do this great wickedness, and sin against God?" It was Joseph's present consciousness of living before the face of God that was the

foundation to him nobly resisting Mrs. Potiphar's entice-
ments to wickedness.

Conversely, the first step into any sin, when there is a
definite inducement to sin, is the eradication of our sense
of the immediate presence of God. Think about it. Many
of the sins we commit would be prevented or stopped by
simply the presence of another human being. If you are
having a spat with your wife, what happens when a fellow human being, not even necessarily a Christian, comes
to the door? The presence of another person is enough
to check your words, and suddenly you can become very
sweet. Or you could be cheating at school and think that
nobody sees you. As soon as the teacher stands over your
shoulder, however, you stop. Why? Because of the presence
of another person. What effect would it have on us if we
had an all-pervasive sense of the presence of God? We see
what it did for Joseph. It kept him from sin.

God's Presence a Restraint against Sin

This is why, even in the New Testament, when we are
called to live lives of ethical and moral purity, we are called
to live such lives motivated by the fear of God. We see this
in Paul's letter to the Corinthians: "Therefore, having these
promises, beloved, let us cleanse ourselves from all filthiness of the flesh and spirit, perfecting holiness in the fear of
God" (2 Cor. 7:1). We are to carry our holiness or sanctification toward perfection in the climate of the fear of God,
a climate that has as one of its indispensable elements this
all-pervasive sense of the presence of God. Why should I
strive to cleanse myself from every defilement of spirit?

Because God is here. He sees and knows and is grieved with whatever is unlike Him and is a contradiction of His holy character. He is not "out there somewhere," but, as He says at the close of the previous chapter, "I will dwell in them and walk among them. I will be their God, and they shall be my people" (2 Cor. 6:16). And Paul says in the light of such promises, "Let us carry our holiness and sanctification on to perfection in the climate of the fear of God."

The fear of God is the chief part of knowledge. That fear is first founded on right views of God's character, and, second, it is constructed of this all-pervasive sense of His presence. Do you know something of this fear? If you are a Christian, then surely your heart cries out in thanks to the Lord for the precious little you know. Isn't this the explanation for so much of our shoddy living and so much of our spiritual deficiency? We have conveniently learned how to limit the effect of the Grand Canyon to those facts we have learned from the books and pictures of that majestic work of God's creation and providence. We don't make our way into the canyon itself and drink in its massive majesty until it takes our breath away.

A Constraining Awareness of Our Obligations to God

The third essential ingredient of the fear of God is what I am calling *a constraining awareness of one's obligations to God.* In other words, to live in the fear of God is not just to know who He is and that He is here. It is also to recognize that in any circumstance in which I find myself, the most important issue is my present obligations to this great God who is here.

Again, consider thoughtfully the sagacious words of Murray: "The fear of God implies our constant consciousness of [our] relation to God, that, while we are also related to angels, demons, men, and things, our primary relationship is to God and all other relationships are determined by, and to be interpreted in terms of, our relation to him…. The first thought of the godly man in every circumstance is God's relation to him and it, and his and its relation to God."[2]

This point can be illustrated using the setting of a church worship service. As you sit in the pew and worship God, you are sustaining relationships to angels (1 Cor. 11:10; Heb. 1:13–14) and to hostile evil powers (Eph. 6:12; Matt. 13:19). You sustain relationships to other people. You sit next to your spouse, mother, father, brother, sister, friend, or acquaintance. In that setting you are also related to material things. You bear a relationship to the pew or chair on which you are sitting, the hymnal you hold in your hand and the clothes on your back. You have many relationships as you sit and worship God. But if you entered that church building in the fear of God, you came in and sat there with your mind on the relationship that takes precedence over every other relationship, namely, that which you sustain with God. And your concern as you sit there is the answer to these questions: What is God's relationship to me, and what is my relationship to Him? What does He require of me, and am I rendering to Him what He requires of me at this moment? If you are worshiping in the fear of God, the most important relationship for you

---

2. Murray, *Principles of Conduct*, 237–38.

is your relationship to God. Your greatest concern will be whether or not you are fulfilling your obligations to Him.

When you gather for corporate worship, you are necessarily and rightfully conscious that you are part of that community of God's people with whom you are rendering worship to God. Our Lord teaches us that if in that setting we are conscious of a disrupted relationship with a brother or sister, we are to suspend our worship while we seek to rectify that disrupted relationship (Matt. 5:23–24). Similarly, when the apostle Paul was correcting some of the disorders in the church at Corinth, he clearly emphasized the necessity of our being aware of our brothers and sisters when we come to the Lord's Table (1 Cor. 11:33). However, in the order of priorities, our supreme concern in worship must be the relationship we have with God. When it is otherwise, God issues the timeless complaint: "This people honors me with their lips, but their heart is far from me" (Mark 7:6).

The importance of the fear of God and that it includes the conscious concern to discharge our obligations to Him makes this question relevant and vital: What has been and what is presently the most important relationship to you in the act of your worship? Is it your relationship to God, or is it your relationship to your watch that is the most important thing? Do you say to yourself, "Well, I've suffered through three-quarters of this; only another quarter of an hour to go"? Or is your relationship to your father or mother the most important thing? Do you think to yourself, "I'm here because Dad and Mom said I had to be, so I'll suffer through another service"? Or is your relationship to your reputation the most important thing? "I am a member of this church, and if I don't show up people will think I'm unhealthy spiritually—so I'll just show up to keep up appearances." Is that what brought you to church? Do you see how practical this is? What is the most pressing issue to you from the time you walk through the church doors—and even before you actually walk through the doors? If you are walking in the fear of God, if you are coming to worship in the fear of God, then you will be overcome with a constraining awareness of your obligations to God.

The Essence of Our Obligations to God

If an essential ingredient of the fear of God is a constraining awareness of my obligations to Him, what then is the essence of my obligations to God? I believe that all of our obligations to God can be broken down into three headings: to love Him supremely, to obey Him implicitly, and to trust Him completely.

To Love Him Supremely. What is the first and great commandment? What is the sum of all that God requires of us? Our Lord Jesus Christ was asked this question. His answer is in Matthew 22:37–38, where we read, "Jesus said to him, 'You shall love the LORD your God with all your heart, with all your soul, and with all your mind.' This is the first and great commandment." Here I am in God's world sustaining relationships with men, angels, demonic powers, and other things. In all of those relationships, the person who is a true child of God and is walking in the fear of God strives to remember and be constrained by the recognition of his obligations to God. While trusting for salvation only in the one who perfectly kept this great commandment on his behalf, nonetheless, the true believer sincerely seeks to love God supremely.

Consider with me a concrete example of what this may involve in the life of one of God's children. Imagine with me a man who is a consistent, professing Christian. He has recently received a substantial raise in his salary as a reward for his diligent labor and loyalty to the company for which he works. As he drives by a new car dealership each day on his way to work, he cannot help but observe that shiny new car glistening in the showroom. He begins to experience a disposition of covetousness and wishes he had that car— not primarily because purchasing that car would be part of a wise economic decision for him and his family or part of the exercise of a God-honoring stewardship of his monetary increase, but simply because it looks so attractive to him. That car in the showroom has become to this man a concrete example of "the lust of the eyes." He knows getting that car will mean he won't be able to increase his giving to the work of God to a degree commensurate with this year's increase in salary. Oh yes, he knows that God says that we are to honor Him with the firstfruits of all our increase (Prov. 3:9), but he has begun to rationalize that it is his "Christian liberty" to make this increase an exception. He is sorely tempted to love paint, leather, and horsepower more than his God. If he succumbs to that temptation, at that point he is not walking in the fear of God. If he is walking in the fear of God, he will not yield to that temptation to capitulate to an idolatrous attachment to that new car.

Am I saying people shouldn't get new cars? Of course not. The point is that if the motivation to get the car is a love for the car that rivals and supersedes the love he has for God, which ought to be supreme love, and if the love for that car prevents obedience to God, which ought to be implicit obedience, then the man is not walking in the fear of God. When our Lord calls sinners to commit themselves to Him as His disciples, He does so with these searching words: "If anyone comes to Me and does not hate his father and mother, wife and children, brothers and sisters, yes, and his own life also, he cannot be My disciple" (Luke 14:26). He says, "If you come to Me, even legitimate love for yourself, which expresses itself in the desire to preserve yourself, must be sacrificed." A love for Him must take you beyond self-preservation to the point that you see your own life as expendable. Living in the fear of God means that you are committed to love God supremely no matter what the cost, even when it may mean refusing to purchase that new car.

Every true child of God knows that he cannot fully obey the divine mandate to love God with all his heart, mind, soul, and strength. A true Christian knows that he stands in constant need of the ongoing application of the blood of Christ for the sin of not loving God with supreme and undivided affection. At the same time, because he is a child of God walking in the fear of God, he joyfully embraces and seeks to live under the constraints of his obligation to love God supremely. He will not tolerate as a pattern of life any person or thing as a rival deity. Living in the fear of God means living consciously committed to the obligation to love God supremely.

To Obey Him Implicitly. Then, as the proof of that supreme love to God, obeying Him unquestioningly is the second aspect of our obligations to God. Jesus said, "You are My friends if you do whatever I command you" (John 15:14). We must obey the laws of the land; God tells us to do so (Rom. 13:1). We must obey ecclesiastical leadership: "Obey those who rule over you, and be submissive, for they watch out for your souls, as those who must give account. Let them do so with joy and not with grief, for that would be unprofitable for you" (Heb. 13:17). We are to obey our superiors (1 Peter 2:18). But God alone is to be obeyed unquestioningly. And if there is any conflict between the expressed will of God and that of any superior appointed by God (be it civil, ecclesiastical, domestic, or occupational), then Acts 5:29 comes into play: "We ought to obey God rather than men." Notice the word "ought." It is our *obligation*, Peter says, to fear—to obey—God, rather than man. Peter was a man walking in the fear of God. Walking in the fear of God, he said to the ecclesiastical leaders, "I have an obligation that transcends any obligation to obey you men. That obligation is to obey my God."

Perhaps the most beautiful example of obedience in godly fear is to be found in the life of our blessed Jesus Christ Himself. As we saw earlier in this book, Scripture says of our Lord in Isaiah 11:2 that "the Spirit of the LORD shall rest upon Him, the Spirit of wisdom and understanding, the Spirit of counsel and might, the Spirit of knowledge and of the fear of the LORD." The Lord Jesus walked in the fear of God. Just how did the fear of God function in Him? We especially see that He loved the Father supremely when we come to that inner sanctuary of Gethsemane and Golgotha. As the Son of the Father's bosom, He loved and delighted in His conscious communion with the Father. He could say to His Father, "I know that You always hear Me" (John 11:42). But now the Father's plan for the Son demanded that He walk down a path in which He would be stripped of the sensible comfort of the support of God. In Gethsemane, the Father gives to His well-beloved Son further insight to what it will mean for Him who knew no sin to be made sin for us. He would have to give up that which for our Lord Jesus was life itself. Yet the Lord Jesus so walked in the Spirit of the fear of God that His supreme love to the Father caused Him to say, "Nevertheless not My will, but Yours, be done" (Luke 22:42). In these words of our Lord we see a striking example of the second essential element of our obligation to God: unquestioning obedience to Him. Though everything in Him recoils from the horrific realities before him, Scripture says that He "became obedient to the point of death, even the death of the cross" (Phil. 2:8).

We may ask what place the fear of God had in our Lord's wholehearted embrace of the Father's will as revealed in the words He uttered while in the throes of the peculiar agonies of Gethsemane. As the writer to the Hebrews reflects on the agonizing experience of Gethsemane, he writes concerning our Lord: "Who, in the days of his flesh, when he had offered up prayers and supplications, with vehement cries and tears to him who was able to save him from death, and was heard because of *his godly fear*, though he was a son, yet he learned obedience by the things which he suffered" (Heb. 5:7–8, emphasis added).

To Trust Him Completely. The third aspect of our obligation to God is to trust Him completely. "But without faith it is impossible to please Him" (Heb. 11:6). We saw demonstrated in the life of Abraham the constraining awareness of his obligation to love God supremely. Abraham proved that he loved God more than he loved his own son when he took hold of the knife to plunge it into Isaac's breast. He demonstrated that his obligation to love God was supreme.

Of course he was to love Isaac his son. He found this no burden. Loving Isaac was the spontaneous outgoing of his affections as a father. Isaac had been given to him and Sarah when they were past the age when men and women normally have children. There was a natural depth of attachment. There was also love, which had not only a natural stream but also a stream of spiritual identification and of spiritual purpose, because all the covenant promises were to be perpetuated through Isaac. Yet notwithstanding the great depth and many facets of his love toward Isaac, Abraham revealed his determination to love his God supremely, obey Him unquestioningly, and trust Him completely. Thus, Abraham's fear of God, the grace and virtue highlighted by God Himself after Abraham was willing to offer up Isaac (Gen. 22:12), was manifested in trusting God completely. This fact is underscored very clearly in Hebrews 11:17–18. Here, we are told that it was by faith that Abraham offered up Isaac, and that in offering him up, Abraham was confident that God was able to raise Isaac from the dead. In other words, his fear of God led him to trust in God completely.

This is precisely the thing to which God calls us. He looks at our "Isaacs" and asks, "Do you love Me more than these?" He often calls us to walk in a course that immediately arouses the protesting voice of natural affection. Parents, what are your ambitions for your children? Suppose God were to summon you into His presence right now and gaze into your eyes with those eyes as a flame of fire before which all things are naked and open. Suppose there God were to ask you what you most desired for your children. What would you answer? Could you answer almost without thinking that your one supreme ambition for your children is that they be what *God* wants them to be? If that means God wants to save them at age seven and take them home at age nine, His will be done. If that means He wants to lay hold of them and send them out to labor in the proclamation of the gospel in some obscure place and to die there in poverty—total failures in the eyes of the world and even of much of the professing church—so it should be. Could you answer that way? If not, my dear parent, your reluctance may be an indication that in this area of your relationship to your children you are not walking in the fear of God. You are not loving Him supremely and trusting Him completely with respect to the future of your children.

Some young people who are reading these pages may have a deep and intimate relationship with their parents. The time may come when, in the ordinary ways by which He makes His will known to His children, God may be saying to some young person, "This is where you must go, and this is what you must do." The young man or woman may be tempted to say, "But, Lord, if I do that, Mom and

Dad won't understand. Mom and Dad may turn against me." If God puts you in such a spot, what are you going to do? At that point you need to ask God, by His Spirit, to so flood your heart with His fear that you will be constrained by the consciousness that your essential and primary and supreme obligation is to Him, and to Him alone. You must not love father or mother more than God, or you will prove yourself unworthy of being His disciple (see Matt. 10:37). There may be times when the only way you can walk down the pathway of the will of God is to step on your own father and mother's heart. You may have to do it with tears. You may have to do it with the sense of inner grief. But do it you must, if you are to walk down the path of the revealed will of God, trusting God to resolve the consequences of your obedience in His way and time.

As with all these other aspects of the evidence of the fear of God at work in the lives of God's people, we find in our Lord Jesus the clearest example of how the fear of God produced absolute confidence and trust in God. Gethsemane and Golgotha were not only the greatest tests of our Lord's obedience rooted in the fear of God. In the midst of that supreme love to the Father and that unquestioning obedience, our Lord's trust in the Father was put to its deepest test. Someone has said that our Lord's last words on the cross, "Father, into Your hands I commit My spirit" (Luke 23:46), were perhaps the greatest act of faith ever exercised on God's earth. Here, with no present sensible delight of the Father's countenance, the heavens shrouded in blackness, the Son of God having experienced within Himself the Father's wrath and displeasure against the sins of His people, in that dark situation, Jesus Christ displayed complete trust in God. Isaiah 50:10 prophesies, "Who among you fears the LORD? Who obeys the voice of His Servant? Who walks in darkness and has no light? Let him trust in the name of the LORD and rely upon his God." As the Lord Jesus spoke His last words, this prophecy was perhaps more fully realized than at any other point in human history. Here was the Servant of God, who obeyed the voice of God, walking in darkness. Yet He so stays Himself on His Father and on the certainty of the Father's promise that He says, "Father, into Thy hands I commit My spirit."

Prior to actually experiencing the events connected with His death, our Lord had repeatedly told the disciples that He would not only be rejected, betrayed, and put to death, but after three days He would rise from the dead. When He bows His head while hanging on the cross and breathes His last, committing His spirit into the hands of His loving Father, He does so in the confidence of faith that He would be raised from the dead.

The Christian's Obligations and the Fear of God

In light of these things we have seen thus far, we should not be surprised to find the fear of God often joined immediately to calls for obedience. Notice how the Lord joins fear, obedience, and love in Deuteronomy 10:12–13: "And now, Israel, what does the LORD your God require of you, but to fear the LORD your God, to walk in all His ways and to love Him, to serve the LORD your God with all your heart and with all your soul, and to keep the commandments of the LORD and His statutes which I command you today for your good?"

Similarly, Philippians 2:12 says, "As you have always obeyed...work out your own salvation with fear and trembling." Child of God, would you grow more in the fear of God and walk in that fear? Then you and I must constantly remind ourselves of this fact. At this moment and in my present circumstances—and, in fact, at any given moment and in whatever my circumstances—the most important thing is my relationship to God and what He requires of me in that circumstance. This God, glorious in Himself; this God who made me; this God who redeemed me—this God is the one to whom I owe the allegiance of unrivaled love, the response of loving obedience, and the trust of unwavering faith.

Therefore, when the price of keeping the smile of your boss at your place of work is such that you are expected to pare off a little corner of truth in a particular business deal, you must not do it. Why not? Because of your obligation to the God who has commanded you to speak only the truth (Eph. 4:25). Do you see the ethical implications? A young man may be facing a great temptation to fulfill his lustful desires. Everything in him may cry out for the gratification of his physical appetite with the young woman he is courting. His passions cry out, "Gratify me!" and his flesh cries out, "Indulge me!" In that situation, his God says, "Flee also youthful lusts" (2 Tim. 2:22), and "Flee sexual immorality" (1 Cor. 6:18). It is the constraining sense of the supremacy of his obligations to God and his unwavering trust that

God in Jesus Christ will give him grace that will enable him to resist this temptation and do the will of his Lord.

We must constantly remind ourselves of the fact that in whatever relationship and whatever circumstances we find ourselves, our obligations to God are supreme. We must constantly remind ourselves what obedience to God involves. We must constantly seek to enlarge the scope of our understanding of what He requires by meditating on and searching out His precepts in His Word. And we must constantly pray for grace to forget all else that would blind us to these realities.

Dear reader, if you are not a Christian, here is the explanation for why you live the way you do. Romans 3:18 says of unconverted people, "There is no fear of God before their eyes." Why do you live the way you live? Because you have no profound sense of the greatness of God's person, no pervasive sense of His presence, and no constraining awareness of your obligations to Him. That is why you find it so easy to cheat at school or in the workplace. That is why you can lie to your parents. That is why you can open your mouth and curse. That is why you can give your body to sensual indulgence. This is why you have chosen to "live unto yourself" (2 Cor. 5:15). Why? I repeat: It is because you have no profound sense of the majesty of God's person, no pervasive sense of His presence, and no constraining awareness of your obligations to Him.

My unconverted reader, you will go on that way until God is pleased to give you a new heart. Jeremiah 32:39–40 says that in the new covenant, God's work is to put His fear within our hearts that we may not depart from Him. The

Holy Spirit never comes into the heart of a man or woman, boy or girl, but as *the Spirit of the fear of the Lord*. If you have no fear of the Lord, it is because you are devoid of the Holy Spirit. If anyone does not have the Spirit of Christ, Scripture says, "He is not his" (Rom. 8:9). The indwelling of the Holy Spirit is a reality that you cannot conjure up. You cannot just repeat a ritualized prayer to obtain this reality. The God of grace and mercy who has treasured up in His Son all that is necessary for the salvation of men bids you look to Him through His Son. He bids you cry to Him so that in grace He would be pleased to give you a new heart and grant you the Spirit who is the Spirit of the fear of the Lord. Ezekiel 36:25–25 contains another wonderful promise concerning the manifold blessings imparted to sinners in the new covenant. However, after clearly stating what He is committed to do in imparting these blessings, God then says, "I will also let the house of Israel inquire of Me to do this for them" (36:37).

Questions for Reflection and Discussion

1. What three things constitute the essential ingredients of the fear of God?

2. What aspect of the attributes of God is particularly highlighted in producing the fear of God?

3. How was this attribute brought to its fullest display in the death of our Lord Jesus Christ?

4. How does the sense of the presence of God contribute to producing the fear of God? Give several biblical examples.

5. What things constitute the essence of our fundamental obligations to God?

6. In what way did our Lord Jesus Christ exemplify this aspect of the fear of God?

◆

CHAPTER FOUR

Source of the Fear of God

A careful student of Scripture from a past generation has written that "it is well known that the fear of God is used to signify not only the whole of His worship but all godly affections whatsoever, and consequently the whole of true religion." This writer could say that it is commonly understood by anyone who knows his Bible that the fear of God can be used as a synonym for the "whole of true religion." I believe that a study of Scripture leads to that conclusion. But that fact also contains a frightening and terrible negative implication. If the fear of God is synonymous with the whole of true religion, then the absence of the fear of God is indicative of the absence of true religion.

We have asked and then answered from the Scriptures a number of crucial questions pertaining to this important subject of the fear of God. But another useful question we may ask regarding the fear of God is, where does it come from? What, according to Scripture, is the source of the fear of God? Suppose your child had never seen a delicious, moist chocolate cake, but you have just baked such a cake and set it in front of him. He asks you what it is, and you respond that it is a cake, something delicious to eat. He asks you what it is made of, and you list the ingredients: flour, shortening, baking powder, cocoa, and so on. You have told him not only what it is but also what makes it what it is. You have told him what the ingredients are. He may next ask where the ingredients came from. You explain that the flour came from grain that is grown out in the field, and the shortening came from either grain or a certain animal that fed upon the field. You are explaining to your child the *origin* of those ingredients.

What we have done in our study thus far is to explain what the cake is—or in our case, what the fear of God is. It is that regard of God which, considering Him in the majesty and glory of His person and the grace manifested in His saving work, produces in us the conviction that His smile is the greatest of life's blessings, and His frown the greatest of life's curses. We have also identified three ingredients of the fear of God. As we consider where those ingredients come from, we must bear in mind that this inquiry is not a mere academic exercise. One of the most crippling errors in all religious experience is to be content with ignorance concerning the origin of virtue. Remember what Paul said of his fellow Jews. They knew that righteousness was necessary in order to be saved. But Paul said of them that, "being ignorant of the righteousness of God, and seeking to establish their own, they did not submit to God's righteousness" (Rom. 10:3). They knew they had to have righteousness, but they weren't concerned to find out what was the source or the origin of the righteousness that alone is acceptable to God.

It is not enough simply to know that you must have the fear of God and the things that constitute that fear. You must know where to get it. Crippling harm can come to you if you don't know where to get the fear of God. This is a matter of great spiritual concern. What is the origin or source of the fear of God? First we will see that the fear of God implanted in the heart is a promised blessing of the new covenant. Second, we will note from Scripture how the fear of God is planted in the heart by the work of God's grace.

A Promised Blessing of the New Covenant

First, then, let us establish from Scripture that the implanting of the fear of God in the heart is a promised blessing of the new covenant. All of God's dealings with men are on the basis of His covenantal relationship to them. In these covenants, God pledges to do certain things on certain conditions that He Himself determines. The blessings of salvation from sin and its consequences come to us within the terms of what Scripture calls the "everlasting covenant" (Heb. 13:20), described sometimes under the term the "new covenant" when it is contrasted with the Mosaic covenant. In Hebrews 8:6–13, God makes it abundantly clear that the blessings purposed and conveyed under the new covenant far exceed the blessings promised and conveyed in the old covenant. This reality is captured in the summary statement of verse 13, where we are told, "In that He says, 'A new covenant,' He has made the first obsolete. Now what is becoming obsolete and growing old is ready to vanish away." When He instituted the Lord's Supper, Jesus said, "This cup is the new covenant in My blood" (1 Cor. 11:25). In other words, all that He is about to accomplish in the shedding of His blood has reference to the blessings to be secured and applied within the framework of the new covenant. No man receives any blessing of the covenant apart from the blood that Jesus shed, but all who receive any benefits from that blood receive them in terms of the specific blessings promised in the new covenant.

What blessings were promised in that covenant? Several blessings are specified in the prophecies of the new covenant in Ezekiel 36 and Jeremiah 31 and 32. We know that these passages refer to blessings to be enjoyed under the new covenant, especially based on Hebrews 8 and 10. We will focus our attention on Jeremiah 32, since it specially addresses the matter of the fear of God and its place in the new covenant.

> They shall be My people, and I will be their God; then I will give them one heart and one way, *that they may fear Me forever*, for the good of them and their children after them. And I will make an everlasting covenant with them, that I will not turn away from doing them good; *but I will put My fear in their hearts* so that they will not depart from Me. Yes, I will rejoice over them to do them good, and I will assuredly plant them in this land, with all My heart and with all My soul (Jer. 32:38–41, emphasis added).

In this context of God promising mercy to His people, He says He will put His fear into their hearts, thus securing their perseverance in His ways. Notice the relationship: "I will put My fear in their hearts so that they will not depart from Me." In the old covenant, even though God set

His law before the people with displays of His majesty and power so that they trembled and dared not even touch the mountain from which He spoke, they still committed spiritual adultery against Him time after time. Eventually, God judged the entire generation who originally received the old covenant by causing everyone in that generation twenty years old and up to die in the wilderness. Eventually, God sent the entire nation into captivity because of their spiritual whoredom. Now, He says, in the administration of this new covenant, all those who come into the blessings of this covenant will not become adulterers against Him. They will not depart from Him, and the reason is this: "I will put My fear in their hearts" (v. 40). That is, "I will so establish My fear in their hearts—that is, in the very seat of their being—that they will cling to Me and to My ways and will not depart from Me."

What do we learn from this statement in Jeremiah's prophecy? We learn first that the fear of God is indeed a blessing of the new covenant. In this age, subsequent to the accomplishment of redemption in the life history of the Lord Jesus, no one truly and rightly fears God unless he has come to possess the fear of God within the framework of the new covenant. Secondly, it is a distinctly sovereign work of God: "I *will put* My fear in their hearts." How can God state any more clearly that He is the one who is going to do this? Also, He says He will put it *in the heart.* What He does will not be a surface thing that will merely affect His people for a time, as in the administration of the Mosaic economy. The pattern of the nation as a whole under the old covenant was of spiritual whoredom and turning from God continually. Jeremiah the prophet declared, "All these nations are uncircumcised, and all the house of Israel are uncircumcised in the heart" (Jer. 9:26). In his final sermon to the Jews in Jerusalem, Stephen summarized the spiritual condition of national Israel throughout the bulk of its history with these words: "You stiff-necked and uncircumcised in heart and ears! You always resist the Holy Spirit; as your fathers did, so do you" (Acts 7:51). Thankfully, God always had a "remnant according to the election of grace" (Rom. 11:5), a people who were regenerated and indwelt by the Holy Spirit and subsequently governed by the fear of God planted within them. But He says that all who come under the blessings of this new covenant will have His fear implanted in their hearts. This reality will secure their cleaving to Him. *[handwritten: Heb 6/10]* And further, this passage tells us that it will be done in a context of gracious blessing. He says, "I will be their God" (Jer. 32:38); "I will not turn away from doing them good" (v. 40); and, "I will rejoice over them" (v. 41). He will implant His fear within the context of the blessings of grace.

What can we conclude from Jeremiah's prophecy? We can conclude two things. First, there is no way for anyone to be a partaker of the fear of God this side of the work of Christ, who established and ratified the new covenant in His blood. We must have it put into the heart as a promised blessing of the new covenant. No such godly fear is ever found growing in purely Adamic soil. The fear of God is an attitude that will not grow in our hearts by nature. As Romans 3:18 says, speaking of natural men, "There is no fear of God before their eyes." The natural man will never fear God with a fear of awe and veneration that binds him to God in a relationship of love, trust, and filial obedience. Only those who come under the blessings of the new covenant know that kind of fear. Such fear does not come through education; it does not come by spiritual osmosis; nor does it come through bloodlines. It comes only as one enters into the blessings of the new covenant by the gracious sovereign activity of God.

The second conclusion we draw from this passage is that all who are partakers of the blessings of the new covenant will manifest in their lives that the fear of God has been planted in their hearts. There is no such thing as a sinner forgiven by the blood of the covenant who does not fear God. There is no such thing as one who comes to Jesus, the Mediator of the new covenant, and is pardoned, but who then goes on to live a life of indifference to communion with God and as a stranger to living in the fear of God.

A Work in the Heart by the God of Grace

Consider with me now the manner in which the fear of God is imparted to the human heart under the new covenant. I pose this question reverently: Does God simply form a disposition called "the fear of God," plunking it down into the heart of a sinner much like someone puts money in a safe? We must say that God certainly *could* operate in that way. If and when God regenerates an infant or a mentally disabled individual, He does so bypassing the ordinary method of His working in saving grace. But Scripture reveals that God's working in grace ordinarily does not bypass the constitution of human beings. God's work in placing His fear in the human heart does not circumvent the operations of the sinner's mind, affections, and will, but it works behind, under, in, and through them so that often it is difficult to discern our working from His working. It is for this reason that our Lord said to Nicodemus that in the work of regeneration the ways of the Spirit are like the operations of the wind—that is, there is an element of mystery, just as there is with the origin and destiny of the wind.

Paul says in Philippians 2:13, "For it is God who works in you both to will and to do for His good pleasure." This text says that God "works in you." When God works in us, we do not just become puppets at the end of a string that God is manipulating, so that we merely wait for impulses to move us to repent and believe, to pray or to obey His commands. No. God "works in you to *will*," says Paul. Working beneath the level of our consciousness, His working in us is discovered when our wills are found actively choosing what is well pleasing in His sight. When I go to church, all I am conscious of is that I choose to go, that I choose to give myself to pray as the congregation seeks the face of God, that I choose to open my mouth and give vent to my worship and praise in sacred song. But, although I am not conscious of it, in all these activities God is working in me to will and to do of His good pleasure.

But when I ask myself why I choose to go to church, to engage in prayer and praise, I must answer that I do so because God has placed His fear in my heart to the end that I might not depart from His statutes, but that I might choose to do the things that He has revealed to be His will for me.

What then is the first distinct blessing of the new covenant? God says that the first thing He will do is to powerfully and inwardly incline His people to a life of obedience. What He requires of them will not be merely external to them, but He said He will write His law on the heart. There will be an inward affinity to that holy law so that there will be an inclination to keep and obey it. God says, "I will not only set My requirements before them, as I did under the old covenant, but I will also inwardly incline them to a life of obedience." What is that but an awareness of our obligation to God, or what I called the second ingredient of the fear of God? Yes, the law is external to me, telling me what to do. But it is also *within* me, *inclining* me to live a life of obedience to its holy demands.

God Owns His People, and They Own Him

What else does God say He will do? In Jeremiah 32:38, He says, "They shall be My people, and I will be their God." "All that I am as I have revealed Myself"—and we know from our perspective in the new covenant that that takes in all that He has revealed in the person and work of His Son— "they will gladly own as theirs." And He says not only that He will be their God, but they will be His people. They will not only own Him as He has revealed Himself, but He will own them. What is this but God bringing Himself into an intimate covenant relationship to His people, filling them with a pervasive sense of His presence and of their relationship to Him and His to them? And isn't that the second ingredient of the fear of God? A penitent and believing sinner recognizes that this great, mighty, transcendent, holy, powerful God is not simply a God out there somewhere, but He is now my God, and I am His child. I belong to Him, and He belongs to me in this covenantal relationship. This is what God has pledged in the new covenant.

True Knowledge of God

And what else does He promise? In Jeremiah 31:34 He says, "No more shall every man teach his neighbor, and every man his brother, saying, 'Know the LORD,' for they all shall know Me, from the least of them to the greatest of them, says the LORD."

God says that in the new covenant He will impart a true and inward knowledge of Himself to His people. Under the old economy there were some who truly knew God, but the great masses of the physical seed of Abraham did not know Him. They saw mighty demonstrations of His power firsthand, but they were utterly ignorant of His heart. God had told them, "I hear your groaning down there in Egypt. I am moved with pity and compassion, so I've sent Moses to be a deliverer to bring you out." But they are no sooner out of Egypt at the shore of the Red Sea, and what do they do? They come to Moses and say, "God brought us out to kill us!" They did not know Jehovah. The truth is that they found themselves standing at the shore of the Red Sea precisely because God heard their cries and had compassion on them and desired to deliver them. But they turn around and say, "He brought us out to kill us!" How would you feel as a father if you told your son, "I've planned a wonderful day for you. We are going to one of your favorite places to do some of your favorite things."

But as soon as you get into the car, your son says, "Are you going to run this car off a cliff and kill me?" You'd say to him, "Son, you don't know me. I've told you what my plans are." The Jews as a nation did not know God. A remnant did, but the rest did not know Him.

God says, in the new covenant, they will not need to be tutoring one another, saying, "Know the Lord," for one of the blessings of the new covenant will be the impartation of a true, saving, and inward experiential knowledge of God. And what is that but right views of the character of God, inwardly and spiritually perceived and loved? Thus, the three ingredients of the fear of God are all here. God says, "I will put these things into their hearts." And when the three ingredients are in the heart, there you have the fear of God.

The Forgiveness of Sins and the Fear of God

There is one statement in this passage to which I have made no reference, and it is, in effect, the very foundational blessing of the new covenant on which all of the other blessings rest and from which they are derived. It is the statement "For I will forgive their iniquity, and their sin I will remember no more" (Jer. 31:34). In other words, the basis on which all these other blessings rests is the blessing of the full and final forgiveness of sins. With these words of promise, God is saying, in essence, "All of these things that I said I would do—inclining you to do My will, giving you an experiential knowledge of Myself, owning you as My people so that you may own Me as your God—all of this," God says, "is inseparably joined to the forgiveness of sins." Only he who receives that forgiveness will know the other blessings

of the new covenant implanted in his heart. Jeremiah saw—
because God revealed it to him—an inseparable relationship
between possessing the fear of God and being in a state of
forgiveness through the blood of the new covenant.

There is a text of Scripture that profoundly and beautifully ties these two thoughts together. In Psalm 130, the
psalmist is in a state of dejection. He is in a spiritual condition that he describes as "the depths." The psalm opens
with the words, "Out of the depths I have cried to You,
O LORD" (v. 1). We are given in the context an indication
as to what those "depths" are. "If You, LORD, should mark
iniquities, O Lord, who could stand?" (v. 3). These words
indicate that the "depths" in which the psalmist found himself were composed of a profound conviction of sin and the
realization that if God were to deal with his sin in strict
justice, it was all over for him. He is conscious that, if such
a holy God should take account of every sin he has committed, he could never abide in God's presence or stand in
the judgment (cf. Ps. 1:5). And if we cannot stand before
God with delight, we cannot walk in His fear. How can
you hold delightful communion with a God before whom
you sense nothing but dread and terror? Who could stand
before God in such a state? That is the haunting question
raised by the psalmist.

Verse 4 provides the answer to his dilemma: "But
there is forgiveness with You, that You may be feared." The
psalmist says, in essence, that no one could stand before the
Lord if He were to mark iniquity and to give us what our
sins justly deserve. And if the psalmist cannot even *stand*
before God, he will know nothing of a heart inclined to do

His will. He will not be able to own God as his God and have God own him as His child. The psalmist will know nothing of this inward experiential acquaintance with God, such that God will delight in him, and he in God. He will know nothing of true godly fear. He can know dread and terror, but he cannot stand before God with reverential awe, delight, and peace.

The answer to this dilemma is that a way of forgiveness has been discovered in God. A Spirit-wrought and believing discovery of God's way of forgiveness will always impart the fear of God in the heart of the one who discovers it. But how is this so? If the text had read, "There is *justice* with God that He may be feared," we could understand that. But there is *forgiveness* with God that He may be feared? How does the discovery of the forgiveness of God secure the fear of God? I suggest that there are two ways in which the experience of forgiveness gives rise to godly fear. A regenerate child of God prior to the coming of our Lord Jesus Christ saw these gospel realities less clearly than we do subsequent to the actual coming of Christ and the sending of the Holy Spirit; but they saw, understood, rejoiced in, and experienced them nonetheless really and truly.

The Display of God's Character

First, in the work Christ performed to secure forgiveness for His people, God has given to us the most concentrated, comprehensive, and glorious display of all His marvelous attributes. If the fear of God begins with right views of God's character, seeing His majesty and His glory, then certainly to discover God's way of forgiveness is to discover the brightest display of all His glorious attributes. Therefore, because there is forgiveness with God, He is feared.

How does that forgiveness relate to the fear of God? Permit me to attempt an answer to that question. We are astounded when we contemplate the wisdom that designed the universe and formed everything in it—everything from the intricacies of a living cell to the expansive galaxies with their multiplied millions of stars. But such contemplations of God's wisdom displayed in these things are like kindergarten knowledge when we stand dumbfounded before the wisdom manifested in the virgin's womb containing and nurturing the incarnate God. It was this same wisdom that conceived the plan and fixed the purpose that sinful men could be forgiven only by God Himself actually becoming a man, the offended God taking the offenses of sinful man on Himself and so discharging those offenses—all so that He might be just and the justifier of those who have faith in Jesus. No wonder Christ is called the wisdom of God (1 Cor. 1:24). What a display of wisdom!

But what about God's holiness? If you had been able to look with Abraham at what was once Sodom and Gomorrah and the other cities of the plain but was now simply a vast cinder going up in smoke "like the smoke of a furnace" (Gen. 19:28), you would have seen God's holiness in a frightening display of His hatred for sin. That display of God's holiness pales in comparison to Gethsemane and Golgotha. It was in the cold night air of Gethsemane that incarnate Deity is given by His Father an amplified understanding of what awaits Him in the coming hours. That understanding causes Him such amazement of heart that He staggers and falls to the ground under the sheer weight of this new insight into what it will mean for Him to become sin for us—to drain the last drop from the cup of God's wrath against the sins of mankind. The intense agonizing session of prayer that followed caused capillaries to burst and mingle blood with His sweat.

We look to the cross, and we see the heavens shrouded in blackness. We look on the heaving bosom of the Son of God, and we hear that piercing cry, "My God, My God, why have You forsaken Me?" (Matt. 27:46). Why was all this necessary? The right answer to that question is that God is so holy, that when the sins of men are laid on His own beloved Son, God must bring down the unrelieved and undiminished stroke of His wrath on His well-beloved Son until He cries out with that cry that eternity will not be able to exegete. God is so holy that He does this even to His dearly beloved Son who had Himself never committed sin. The apostle Paul expressed these realities with the words: "He who did not spare His own Son, but delivered Him up for us all, how shall He not with Him also freely give us all things?" (Rom. 8:32).

To discover the way of forgiveness forged in the terrible agonies of Christ in Gethsemane and Golgotha is to see a display of wisdom and holiness that far outstrips any other display God has made of these attributes. Further, we read in Colossians 2:15 that Christ made a public spectacle of the powers of darkness when He triumphed over them in His death and glorious resurrection. Think of all the powers of hell that would have sought to keep Him in a state of death. But Peter says that "it was not possible that He should be held by [death]" (Acts 2:24).

Then, there is the display of God's love. Who can fathom it? "But God demonstrates His own love toward us, in that while we were still sinners, Christ died for us" (Rom. 5:8). The cross is the crowning display of the majestic, loving condescension of the Son of God. For this reason the apostle Paul could write the following words: "And being found in appearance as a man, He humbled Himself and became obedient to the point of death, even the death of the cross" (Phil. 2:8). Do you see how the discovery with spiritual understanding of the way of forgiveness produces the fear of God? How can a rational creature discover those things without standing amazed before such a God? How can one contemplate such realities and not be overcome with wonder, awe, and a newly born conviction that a God who would do such things in His relentless pursuit of our salvation is worthy of our hearts' undivided affection and the unrivaled submission of our will to His will?

Peace with God and Filial Fear

The second reason why forgiveness and the fear of God are joined is that a believing reception of the forgiveness God offers through His Son brings deliverance from the dominating influence of the fear of dread and terror that so often accompanies conviction of sin. When a sinner is forgiven by God, the dominating fear of dread and an aversion to God is exchanged for a reverential, love-compelled fear and submission of an adopted son. The apostle Paul affirms of all believers: "For you did not receive the spirit of bondage again to fear, but you received the Spirit of adoption by whom we cry out, 'Abba, Father'" (Rom. 8:15). Who can discover and embrace this kind of love and not instinctively respond by saying, "Here, Lord, I give myself away, 'Tis all that I can do"? God, by showering mercy on the undeserving and extending forgiveness to the sinner, brings him out of a state of the fear of terror and into a condition of reverent, filial fear. It is this reality John is addressing when he writes, "There is no fear in love; but perfect love casts out fear, because fear involves torment. But he who fears has not been made perfect in love" (1 John 4:18). This verse was not put in our Bibles in order to cancel the massive biblical witness to that fear of God which is "the soul of godliness." Rather, they clearly establish the truth that I have sought to articulate in this paragraph.

Mercy and grace, therefore, combine to elicit the fear of God in a way that all the terrors of the law could never rival. This godly fear considers God's mercies and benefits received, more than His judgments threatened. The fear of dread thinks more of judgment and issues in cringing withdrawal from God. The Spirit-imparted fear of God thinks of mercies given, and it leads to reverential worship and loving communion with God. The fear of God, which is the fruit of mercy received, regards more the open hand of God's blessing than the closed fist of His judgment. It is this reality that enabled the psalmist to declare, "Behold, the eye of the LORD is on those who fear Him, on those who hope in His mercy" (Ps. 33:18).

Forgiveness of Sins Misused

There are several practical implications of this teaching. First, we behold the folly of all man-made religions. Every man-made religion either *seeks to produce the fear of God on some basis other than forgiveness,* or it *promises forgiveness in a way that does not produce the fear of God.* Every scheme to attain the righteousness of God not based on the gospel but on human "wisdom" will fail in one of those two ways. Some will say that we dare not tell people they can be fully accepted and forgiven on the basis of the doing and the dying of another, because those who believe this will live a lawless life. That's the argument of the Roman Catholic Church. They don't dare teach free and full forgiveness; otherwise, they reason, people will think they can sin with impunity. They believe that the way to produce the fear of God that results in obedience is to rub the conscience raw with terrors and insecurity and doubts about one's acceptance with God. Then the person will fearfully attempt to obey God, hoping he will do well enough to obtain God's favor. But what we have seen about the way God produces His fear in the heart of man exposes Romanism for what it is—a false religion proclaiming what Paul describes as "another gospel," which, in reality, is no gospel at all. In stark contrast to this Romish heresy, God takes the raw conscience full of the terrors of a deserved damnation and, disclosing the way of forgiveness in the person and work of Christ, binds that believing heart to Himself in a reverential fear that is suffused with love and trust.

The second type of false religion operates in an almost opposite manner. Its proponents affirm that through the

blood of the cross sinners indeed receive complete forgiveness, and having (once *professed*) a reception of that
forgiveness—by "praying the sinner's prayer" or "making a
decision for Christ"—nothing they subsequently do can
take them out of God's favor. Many of those who receive
such a message are utterly devoid of the fear of God. They
show little if any concern to walk before Him with a sensi-
tive conscience. They don't know what it is to be powerfully
inclined to obedience to God's holy law from the heart.
They have no fear whatsoever. They don't tremble the
way many poor Roman Catholics do, wondering if maybe
they'll wake up in purgatory tomorrow. They are absolutely
certain they are going to wake up in heaven because they
are forgiven through the blood of the cross. Yet their lives
manifest a total lack of the fear of God. They desecrate
God's holy day, giving Him a token hour or two and use
the rest of the day as they please with no reference to His
law. They order their homes and their time and the use of
their televisions and other digital toys with no reference to
God's law. Why? Because they have believed a lie—that
they could have their sins forgiven, yet remain strangers to
the fear of God, both in its roots and its fruits.

Both of those errors are damning at the core. You can't
fear God as you ought until you come into the blessedness
of full forgiveness. But if you come into that blessedness,
you *must* fear Him. If you don't, you have never truly experienced the saving mercy of God.

Practical Words of Instruction

Do you have a conscience that has been rubbed raw? Have the terrors of the law and of God tracked you down? Do you have a fear of dread, but know nothing of the fear that is based on forgiveness? Do you have the spirit of bondage, but know nothing of the Spirit of adoption that makes you cry, "Abba, Father"? If this is your condition, you must understand that you will find no rest and no true fear of God until you come, just as you are, to Jesus. He is the Mediator of the new covenant, and He is seated on the mercy seat, and it is at the mercy seat that there is a way of forgiveness that He may be feared. You will not fear Him until you entrust yourself to Him as your Savior and your Lord. Cast yourself on Him just as you are—for that is how He bids you to come—and He will receive you. The enemies of our Lord Jesus accused Him in a pejorative way that unwittingly captured a glorious truth: "This Man receives sinners" (Luke 15:2).

There is also a word of consolation for troubled souls. There are true children of God who feel themselves so sinful that, at times, they wonder how it can be that God bears so long with them. If that is your condition, don't listen to the people who tell you just to forget your sin and rejoice in the Lord. No; don't forget your sin. Rather, let the Holy Spirit show you all of your sin that He knows you are able to bear—realizing He has only shown you the one-thousandth part of it. God's Spirit will enable you to say with the psalmist, "If You should mark iniquity, who could stand?" Then, the more you see of your sin, the more you will be amazed at the magnitude of God's glory in providing forgiveness. And the more you see the magnitude of

His glory in providing forgiveness, the more you will fear Him. "But with you there is forgiveness, that you may be feared." Octavius Winslow wrote, "Soak the roots of thy profession daily in the blood of Christ." That's what we all need to do. And as you soak them there and come again and again to Jesus, the Mediator of the new covenant, you will find the fear of God deepening in your heart and more and more regulating the patterns of your life.

There is also in these truths a word of conviction to any who are deceived concerning their true spiritual state and condition. You may feel yourself to be forgiven, while you experience no dread, no fear of hell, because you are persuaded that all is well with your soul. You say, "I have the blessings of the new covenant!" But, the question is, where is the fear of God? God's own Word says that if He has brought you into that covenant, He has put His fear within your heart. Do you display the constraining awareness of your obligations to Him? Does your life manifest that you live with a pervasive sense of His presence? Has your understanding of forgiveness bound you to a life lived in the fear of God? Let me make it more personal. If someone were to ask your children, "What is the one thing that characterizes your mom and dad above everything else?" would they be able to answer, "They fear God"? Would they be able to say, "In everything in the home, Daddy's first concern is always to discover what God says in His Word concerning every issue." Would your children say that the fear of God is a dominant characteristic of their father and mother? The testimony of your children that you live a life characterized by godly fear can't be bought or coerced. It has to be earned, and it is earned by a life actually lived in the fear of God.

Must you admit to yourself that your children—or whoever lives close enough to you to know what makes you tick—could not give that testimony concerning you? If that is the case, call out to God today and plead, "Oh God, give me such a sight of forgiving grace that I will begin truly to fear Thee." The fear of God that marks the true believer begins with forgiveness of sin in the climate of all the gracious provisions of the new covenant.

Questions for Reflection and Discussion

1. Why is it important to know the source of the fear of God?

2. What passages more than others help us to frame a biblical understanding of the source of the fear of God, which is the "soul of godliness"?

3. What blessings are distinctly promised in the administration of the new covenant?

4. What passage of Scripture is helpful in showing the relationship between the forgiveness of sins and the fear of God? How does this passage do this?

5. Why is the predominance of the "fear of dread and terror" inconsistent with the faith that unites us to Christ and to the forgiveness of sins?

6. How does Roman Catholic teaching contradict the biblical teaching concerning assurance of sins forgiven and the fear of God?

7. How does "easy believism" contradict the clear biblical teaching between true forgiveness and the fear of God?

◆

CHAPTER FIVE

Relationship of the Fear of God to Our Conduct

We saw in the last chapter that whenever the fear of God is present, it is because God has applied with power the blessings of the new covenant ratified and sealed by the blood of Christ. The fear of God is thus a blessing that is inseparably joined with joy and the realization of the forgiveness of sins. As Manton has so beautifully said, "The heart is shy of a condemning God, but closeth with and adhereth to a pardoning God; and nothing breedeth this fear to offend so much as a tender sense of the Lord's goodness in Christ."[1] Until a person knows the forgiveness of God based on the blood of the everlasting covenant, he will never rightly fear God. He may be terrified of God; he may have a dread of God; but that terror and dread will drive him away from God. The fear of God couched in the consciousness of forgiveness is a fear that causes us to draw near to God and to cling to Him and His ways.

---

1. Thomas Manton, *The Complete Works of Thomas Manton* (London: James Nisbet & Co., 1872), 7:176.

Now we come to what I am calling the relationship between the fear of God and conduct, and I have two propositions to set forth. The first proposition is that *the fear of God is the holy soil that produces a godly life*. The second proposition is that *the absence of the fear of God is the unholy soil that produces an ungodly life*.

Holy Soil That Produces a Godly Life

What is the practical effect of the fear of God in the life of a child of God? Let us look at several texts of Scripture in which we see men and women under a great variety of circumstances, and yet in each case where there is true godliness, it will be found to be rooted in the soil of the fear of God.

The Example of Abraham

In the first several verses of Genesis 12, we are told that Abraham was called by God to leave his homeland. Later, Genesis 20 finds him sojourning with his wife, Sarah, whom the Scripture says was "a woman of beautiful countenance" (Gen. 12:11). They eventually came to a place called Gerar. Abraham knew that there was a heathen king there, and he also knew something of the practice of heathen kings when they see pretty women. So Abraham reasoned, "If I come into that area and the king sees my wife, he is going to set his desires on her. I will be standing in the way, and therefore he will just dispose of me to get my wife. This is what I will do: I will tell a half-truth; I will say Sarah is my sister." It was a half-truth, which in reality is invariably a full lie. There was a blood relationship there, but Sarah was more than just his half-sister; she was also his wife. The effect of Abraham's lie was that Abimelech took Sarah into his house, but God sovereignly restrained him from engaging in any sexual relationships with her. Then God revealed Himself to Abimelech in a dream and told him, "If you seek to take this woman into your harem you are a dead man!" (Gen. 20:3). So Abimelech went to Abraham and said, "Why did you do this to me?" (Gen. 20:9). Notice Abraham's answer: "Because I thought, surely the *fear of God* is not in this place; and they will kill me on account of my wife" (Gen. 20:11).

Do you see what Abraham is saying? He says, "Abimelech, you asked me for the reason why I was fearful that you would think nothing of killing me and then taking my wife. It is because I reasoned this way. This is a heathen land. You are a heathen king. Since there is no knowledge of the true God in your land, the God who has revealed Himself to me, I assumed that there is no fear of God in this place—because where there are no right views of God, there cannot be any fear of God. And if there is no fear of God, there will be no ethical sensitivity. And since the fear of God is absent, your conduct will be a reflection of the absence of His fear; therefore, I did what I did." Abraham assumed that the only soil out of which godliness could grow was the fear of God. And if that soil were not present, neither would the fear of God be present. This incident in the life of Abraham shows us that very clearly in the history of God's revelation there is an inseparable relationship between the fear of God and practical godliness.

The Example of Joseph

Let us look at another example of this principle as it is found in Genesis 42. Joseph's brothers had come down to Egypt to get grain. Joseph was sitting on the throne, second only to the pharaoh himself. He had accused his brothers of being spies and was "proving" whether or not they were, although he knew all along that they were his own brothers. To convince them that he was a trustworthy and honest man and that his commands were just, notice what he said in verses 18 and 19: "Then Joseph said to them the third day, 'Do this and live, for *I fear God*: If you are honest men, let one of your brothers be confined to your prison house; but you, go and carry grain for the famine of your houses'" (emphasis added).

Joseph says, in effect, "I need give no other reason as a basis for my godly, honest dealings with you than that I am a man in whose heart there is the soil of the fear of God, and out of that soil will grow practical godliness. My fear of God makes me an honest and trustworthy man." Joseph showed that he, like Abraham, understood the principle that the fear of God is the holy soil that produces a godly life.

God Sees All

A somewhat unusual injunction is found in Leviticus 19:14: "You shall not curse the deaf, nor put a stumbling block before the blind, but shall fear your God: I am the LORD." If a person is deaf, he cannot hear you. And if he cannot hear you, can he be hurt by what you say? No. Yet God says, "Don't curse the deaf man." What God is saying is this: "Your conduct with reference to others must not be governed by their ability to retaliate against your wrong-doings. It must not be governed by its impact on your reputation before them. The one principle that is to govern all your conduct with all people in all circumstances and at all times is that My eye is upon you and I see. My ear is open and I hear." Never let your conduct with any person be governed by any lower principle than this: How will God view this conduct? So what if the blind person can't see if you trip him up—God sees it. So what if the deaf person can't hear when you curse him—God hears.

This is why if you are a student who fears God, you won't cheat at school. If you are walking in the fear of God, your teacher could go on a three-hour recess while you are taking your final exam. It would not make a bit of difference whether the teacher was there or not, so far as your honesty is concerned. Even if she were absent, you would put down only what you have learned. You will not sneak a look at the desk next to you; you will not pull out a crib sheet. But what if you are a cheater—a confirmed cheater? That should tell you that you know nothing of the fear of God. So what if the teacher can't see—God sees you! Or what if you are a young man who has two vocabularies—one you use around home and church and the other you use out in the ball field with your buddies. You can curse right along with the rest of them. But you never let your dad or mom hear one such word. What are your dad and mom in comparison to God? Doesn't He hear? He knows each time you swear. He could give you the time, place, occasion, and decibel level of every last curse. If you are content that your

mom and dad don't hear and don't know, then it is an indication that you are not walking in the fear of God.

Adults face the same temptations and the same realities in many situations. Every April we sit down to fill out
our tax returns. We must be as careful to cut no corners
as if every single tax agent from Maine to California were
leaning over our shoulder. Why? Because we fill out that
income tax form in the fear of God. We must be conscious
that what we put on that form must pass the test of the eye
of omniscience, not just the eye of the IRS agents. If you
are able to cheat on your income tax statement and claim
more deductions for the church than you actually gave, and
if this is the pattern of your life, you know nothing of the
fear of God, and God will bring your pattern of thievery
and dishonesty as a witness against you in the day of judgment unless you repent.

It is the fear of God that makes a man in the office or
the shop just as careful to avoid lustful or flirtatious glances
as he would be if his wife were standing at his side, and
she were a righteously jealous woman. If you walk in the
fear of God, you are a man with blinders. There is a check
on your eyes. Why? Because you know it is not ultimately
what your wife sees and what she knows, it is what God
sees and knows that matters, and you are seeking to keep a
heart that is pure before His eyes.

Scripture says of Job that he was a man who "feared
God and shunned evil" (Job 1:1). One of the very specific
and concrete manifestations of Job's fear of God is found
in the words he spoke in Job 31:1, "I have made a covenant with my eyes; why then should I look upon a young

woman?" Any man who is impenitently flirtatious and lustful with his looks and his words *as the pattern of his life* knows nothing of the fear of God. According to the Bible's use of the word, he is an "adulterer" who "will not inherit the kingdom of God" (Matt. 5:27–28; cf. 1 Cor. 6:9).

Consciousness of the Eye of God

Another instructive real-life illustration of how the fear of God operates at a very practical level is found in Nehemiah. In Nehemiah 5:14–15, Nehemiah says to the people:

> Moreover, from the time that I was appointed to be their governor in the land of Judah, from the twentieth year until the thirty-second year of King Artaxerxes, twelve years, neither I nor my brothers ate the governor's provisions. But the former governors who were before me laid burdens on the people, and took from them bread and wine, besides forty shekels of silver. Yes, even their servants bore rule over the people, but I did not do so, because of the fear of God.

Nehemiah says that he did not do what his predecessors did—that is, use a position of assigned leadership as a steppingstone to personal advantage—"because of the fear of God." The basis of his conduct was his consciousness that the eye of God was on him. He recognized that if he used his position for his own advantage, he would forfeit the smile of God. That fact alone was enough to cause Nehemiah to walk in a path in which he refused to take advantage of others for the sake of personal gain.

Isn't that one of the biggest problems in human relationships—people taking advantage of others for personal gain? We often are insensitive to others' needs in the pursuit of fulfilling our own needs and desires. We often are selfish in seeking to live to our own satisfaction while we trample over the needs of others. We are tightfisted in business dealings. We are unreasonable in our expectations as parents. What is the great cure for all of this? It is to be able to say with Nehemiah, "Because of the fear of God." In the most practical way, we again see the crucial place that fear of God is to have in the life of His people.

This God-implanted grace of the fear of God being nurtured by the awareness that the eye of God is on us is equally operative in the New Testament age of an accomplished and Spirit-applied redemption. The moment you, in your Christian life, cease to be governed in every relationship by the thought of your relationship to God in Christ, by the sense of His presence, by the reality of His smile, by the aversion of His frown, then the very nerve that energizes you to press on in holiness is severed. Haven't you found that to be so? What can motivate you when the thought of your relationship to God ceases to grip you? What frown can turn you from evil when the thought of God's frown no longer turns you from it? What smile can induce you to walk in the path of righteousness when God's smile will no longer induce you? There is nothing else that can do it. When you have gotten beyond the constraining and compelling influence of the fear of God, functioning in conjunction with the compelling power of the love of Christ (2 Cor. 5:14), you have gotten beyond the sphere in which holiness can be perfected (2 Cor. 7:1). The only soil out of which godliness grows is the fear of God.

An Eye toward Pleasing God

Consider Colossians 3:22: "Bondservants, obey in all things your masters according to the flesh." Paul says to the Christian slaves present in the church at Colossae, "Though you have a gracious master in heaven, you still have human masters on earth, and you are to obey them in all things. You must not render your obedience coextensive with your personal evaluation of whether what they have required is right and just." "No," he says, "obey them in all things." The only exception is if they command you to do something contrary to the law of God. It is essential that new believers learn that lesson. Any new relationships into which you enter by virtue of faith in Christ do not cancel out the demands of those relationships already existing when you were united to Christ.

Paul knows that there are two different ways that servants might "obey" their masters. They could, first, serve them "with eyeservice, as men-pleasers" (v. 22). But Paul says "*not* with eyeservice, as men pleasers." That is, do not do your work with reference to the master's eye, because in three minutes' time your master may be gone. He will go off to his business in town, and his eye will be gone. Then, what will motivate you to fulfill your assigned tasks? What will cause you to work up a lather performing that very mundane task set before you? You will have lost much of your motivation if you are motivated only by the master's eye.

But there is another way in which servants may "obey" their masters—"in sincerity of heart, fearing God." This is the climate in which Paul urges these Christian slaves to do their work. "In sincerity of heart" means with a heart that is not divided between seeking to be a man pleaser and a God pleaser. It means with a heart that is single in walking and working in the fear of God—"fearing God." Is this to say that the only way a common house slave can do his often mundane work acceptably to God is to do it in the climate of the fear of God? Absolutely. The fear of God is to motivate us within a very broad spectrum of duties, all the way from a king reigning in righteousness to a common house slave scrubbing dirt and dung from an animal pen! Just like the servant, the only way that the king can perform his duties acceptably to God is to perform them in the climate of the fear of God. The same is true for the slave—the eye of the master on earth is not to be the focus of concern, but the focus must be on the eye of the master in heaven.

Practical Implications

Scripture clearly teaches that the only soil out of which a godly life can grow is the soil of the fear of God. What are some of the most important implications of this teaching?

First, *consider the folly of seeking to solve the problems of human conduct without considering the necessity of the fear of God.* God has rooted ethics (human conduct) in religion (man's relationship to God). When you slay true religion, it is only a matter of time before any semblance of ethical integrity will die. Three or four generations ago God was thrown out of our national life, so far as true religion is concerned. In the place of true religion came humanism—the notion that man is god—and liberalism, which "remade" God in the image of man. Even so, some residue of the ethics rooted in true religion still permeated the fabric of the ethics of our country. What has happened in the past fifty to seventy years is that even this residue has been all but obliterated. Now, by and large, people have no thought of God when considering ethical issues. Take the so-called drug problem as an example. It seems that everyone is concerned about the drug problem. Former drug addicts are invited to talk to high school students. Police officers are invited to school assemblies and make an effort to scare the kids away from dabbling in illicit drugs. But what happens? The kids turn them all off. They say they don't want to hear any more. Why? Because people are attempting to attack an ethical problem without facing this principle that the fear of God is the only soil out of which godly living and stable ethics can grow. Paul said it this way in Romans 1:28: "And even as they did not like to retain God in their knowledge, God gave them over to a debased mind."

The second thing to consider is *the relationship between true revival and the ethical and social changes which always follow*. A revival is an extensive and powerful movement of the Spirit of God, performing His ordinary work in a most extraordinarily concentrated way. It is a mighty and sovereign work of God implanting true religion—the fear of God—in the hearts of many people in a given geographical area in a relatively short time. And what happens whenever God works in such a way? What happens in a community of ten thousand people if suddenly one or two thousand

of those people begin to walk in the fear of God? The conduct of those people is no longer governed by the eye of
the policeman but by the eye of God. The students in the
schools conduct themselves not with reference to the teacher's eye but to the eye of God. The community becomes in
great measure a little Eden. Why? Because the fear of God
implanted in the hearts of a number of people begins to be
the soil out of which grows a pattern of community ethical
uprightness. People begin to be kind to one another and
thoughtful of one another. Every genuine Spirit-wrought
revival in history has always been the womb out of which
great social and ethical changes have been birthed.

The third application is that *parents must consider the
basis on which we should evaluate our influence with our children.* There are three great streams of influence on our
children. The first and essential one is the home; the second is the school; and the third is the church. Did I get the
order mixed up? No. You have them under your roof for
the greatest number of hours and therefore have the most
powerful influence. The school has them the next greatest
number of hours (unless they are schooled at home), and
the church has them the fewest.

Do you want to evaluate whether your influence as a
parent is an influence owned of God and is being used as an
instrument in the hands of God? Here is one way to evaluate it: To what extent are your children learning the fear of
God by your example, precepts, and consistent exercise of
biblical discipline of them and by the kind of educational
framework in which you place them? Do your children see
that in all of your conduct, the most forceful and powerful

influence on you is the eye of God? Or do they see you living two or three different kinds of lives—one in church, one with a certain group of friends, one with another circle of friends? By your example and precepts, are you teaching your children the fear of God? If not, don't be shocked if they become cynical toward the truth of God's Word and the salvation which you say you possess, but which has not produced in you a life lived in the fear of God "all day long" (Prov. 23:17).

Every godly parent should constantly be pleading with his children in the words of David: "Come, you children, listen to me; I will teach you the fear of the LORD" (Ps. 34:11). However, Scripture and pastoral sensitivity demand a very vital qualifying word at this point in our study. In Proverbs 1:7 we read, "The fear of the LORD is the beginning of knowledge, but fools despise wisdom and instruction." The first chapter of Proverbs, which begins with a powerful commendation of the fear of God, ends with a very sobering description of the man or woman who came to years of discretion and rejected all of the training he or she had received concerning the fear of God. Solomon states it this way:

> Then they will call on me, but I will not answer;
> They will seek me diligently, but they will not find me.
> Because they hated knowledge
> *And did not choose the fear of the LORD,*
> They would have none of my counsel
> And despised my every rebuke.
> Therefore they shall eat the fruit of their own way,

And be filled to the full with their own fancies.
(Prov. 1:28–31; emphasis added)

In these very sobering words, there is no hint that
the son or daughter who refused to be governed by the
fear of God did so because of the inconsistency of his or
her parents. Rather, the fault is laid squarely at the feet of
the young man or woman who "hated knowledge and did
not choose the fear of the Lord." The Bible does record
that some parents miserably failed in teaching the fear of
God to their children by precept, discipline, and example,
thereby materially influencing the subsequent ungodliness of their children. A tragically classic example of this
is found in the record concerning Eli (1 Sam. 2:27–30).
However, nowhere does the Bible teach that the wayward
child of a Christian parent necessarily points to and infal-
libly proves that the state of such children is a witness to
parental failure to live in and instruct their children concerning the fear of God. To buttress this qualification I
quote Jehovah's words spoken through Isaiah the prophet:
"I have nourished and brought up children, and they have
rebelled against me" (Isa. 1:2). Would any dare to charge
God with parental delinquency?

Evaluate along this same line the influence of the school
your children attend. If God says that the fear of God is
the chief part of knowledge, then I think it is right to say
that the absence of the fear of God is the chief part of folly.
And if that is true, many children are under calculated folly
day in and day out in their public or state school system.
They are taught that life can be lived without reference to

the fear of God. You may say there is no teacher that ever says that. But by the very absence of any attempt to teach any standard of ethics and morality rooted in the fear of God, they are saying the fear of God is not needed.

This is how you ought to evaluate the influence of the church as well: Does my church teach my children the fear of God, or does it just keep them busy and happy? Does it teach the true character of God? Does it seek by the grace of God to implant in young people the sense of His presence and requirements of His holy law and wonders of His grace as revealed in the gospel? That is the measure by which to evaluate the church's influence. We must evaluate it not only with reference to our young people but with reference to ourselves. What do the hymns we sing teach us? What kind of spiritual climate does the church promote in its gatherings for public worship? Does it promote and seek to maintain the fear of God?

I recently communicated with a dear friend of mine engaged in pastoral labor in Australia. In my letter, I asked him to give me an update on the condition of the church he has faithfully served for many years. In response, amid some very encouraging things, he mentioned a major discouragement in conjunction with some people leaving the church. He said that for some of these their motive for leaving was their "concern that young Johnny is not getting ministered to in the *lingua franca* of infantile babble, or, entertained with the ditties and jingles of upbeat rhythm." May God have mercy on spineless and foolish parents who will leave a bastion of solid biblical preaching, God-centered and reverential worship, and vital congregational love and mutual

service by capitulating to Johnny's whining desire for "infantile babble…with the ditties and jingles of upbeat rhythm."
The fear of God is the soil out of which a godly life grows,
and it is only in the soil of the fear of God that true godliness will ever be found. The home, school, and church must
with united example and instruction seek to rear the rising
generation in that which is the chief part of knowledge.

Unholy Soil That Produces an Ungodly Life

If the fear of God is the soil out of which a godly life grows,
then may we not assume that it is true to say that the
absence of the fear of God is the unholy soil out of which
an ungodly life grows? However, we need not rely on a mere
assumption to prove this proposition; it can be demonstrated from Scripture. We will do this first by considering
in some depth a key text that will set the framework for
this part of our study. Second, we will look at several specific passages that support the conclusions taken from this
main text. Then, we will draw out some further practical
conclusions and observations.

A Key Text: Romans 3:18

A key text to demonstrate this proposition that *the absence
of the fear of God is the unholy soil which produces an ungodly
life* is Romans 3:18: "There is no fear of God before their
eyes." This quotation from the Old Testament wraps up a
string of scriptural proofs given by Paul to establish the uni-
versal sinfulness of men before God, and why it is that all
men without exception desperately need the salvation that
is to be found in Christ alone and received by faith alone.

He says that the underlying cause for the ungodliness of the whole world is that "there is no fear of God before their eyes." The absence of the fear of God is the cause of a disordered, ungodly life, such as Paul describes in Romans 3:10–18.

The ungodly, as they view and live life, as they carry out their desires and ambitions, do so devoid of the fear of God. When someone has just had his picture taken with a flash camera, he will have a bright spot before his eyes for the next minute or two. Everything he looks at will appear to have that bright spot superimposed on it. He can't look at his hand, a tree, a house, or another person without seeing the spot. It is continually "before his eyes." But the Scripture says of the wicked, "There is no fear of God before their eyes." That is, when they get up in the morning and contemplate the coming day, they look out at life without having superimposed on their moral vision the being of God, the claims of God, the character of God, the salvation of God, the law of God, and the judgment of God. They go out into that day with no fear of God superimposed on their life. That is Paul's accusation. Therefore, the apostle tells us, when you see the kind of life the ungodly live, this is the explanation behind it. This is the reason that the life of the ungodly is so depraved and sinful: "There is no fear of God before their eyes."

The godly man is the man who, in everything, has the "bright spot" of the fear of God before his eyes. He can't think of the day before him without reflexively considering, "This is the day that the Lord has made. I am His servant. He is my God. So as I go out into this day, into the shop, school, or office, as I work or engage in conversation, everything must have stamped on it the reality of God's being, my relationship to Him, His claims on me, and His provision for me." The fear of God is before his eyes, and it colors every facet of his life. Conversely, the ungodly man is the man who does not have this fear of God before his eyes. He has no regard to God's authority, no consideration of God's law, no serious concern regarding God's offered salvation, and no concern to have God's smile, nor does he dread God's frown.

We learn at the very outset, therefore, that moral and ethical problems, problems of life and conduct, are rooted in divinely revealed principles and precepts. You cannot separate ethics, morality, and conduct from true biblical religion. You cannot do it, for God has joined them. What God has joined together, man attempts to put asunder only to his own peril. It is clear from Romans 3:18 that the absence of the fear of God is indeed the unholy soil out of which the ungodly life grows.

Having looked at Romans 3:18 as a basic point of reference, let us consider two other supporting and explanatory texts in the Old Testament—first, Psalm 10. The context of this psalm is set out very clearly in the first two verses:

> Why do You stand afar off, O LORD?
> Why do You hide in times of trouble?
> The wicked in his pride persecutes the poor;
> Let them be caught in the plots which they have
>   devised.

Here we see the righteous being oppressed and pursued by the wicked, and it seems as though God doesn't care.

This is a great problem that surfaces again and again in the Psalms. It is a problem we experience as Christians. There are times when we say, "God, this doesn't seem right." What would you think of me as a father if I could see my son kicked around and abused by a bully, and I had the power to do something, but I did nothing? Wouldn't you have some questions about the depth of my love to my child? Of course you would. God's people also have this problem.

In that context, the psalmist demonstrates what happens in the mind of the wicked when he observes this. He picks on the righteous, but no thunderbolts break out of heaven, and no lightning strikes him. So he is made bold to go on in his wickedness. Notice, first, what the wicked man does:

> His ways are always prospering;
> Your judgments are far above, out of his sight;
> As for all his enemies, he sneers at them.
> He has said in his heart, "I shall not be moved; I shall never be in adversity."
> His mouth is full of cursing and deceit and oppression;
> Under his tongue is trouble and iniquity.
>
> He sits in the lurking places of the villages;
> In the secret places he murders the innocent;
> His eyes are secretly fixed on the helpless.
> He lies in wait secretly, as a lion in his den;
> He lies in wait to catch the poor;
> He catches the poor when he draws him into his net.
> So he crouches, he lies low,
> That the helpless may fall by his strength.
> (Ps. 10:5–10)

The wicked carries out all his schemes against the righteous, the poor, and the helpless. But this section of the psalm is bounded by verses 4 and 11, both of which tell us *why* the wicked does what he does. Notice the reason for all of this in verse 4: "The wicked in his proud countenance does not seek God; God is in none of his thoughts." In other words, the wicked man evacuates his mind of conscious thoughts of God. That doesn't mean he is an outspoken atheist. But it means that God does not enter into the thoughts that govern his life. All his *thoughts* are that there is no God. He makes his plans; he carries out his ambitions. But he does so without any reference to God. Verse 11 shows that the same wicked man seeks to rid himself of any constraining awareness of the character of God: "He has said in his heart, 'God has forgotten; He hides His face; He will never see.'" He tries to limit God's omniscience. Why does he push God out of his thoughts? And when he can't fully succeed in that, why does he seek to pervert and limit the character and ability of the God who remains in his thoughts? He does this because he cannot live an ungodly life unless he can keep himself out of the orbit of the fear of God. So if he is to grow his plants of ungodly living, he must condition the soil until it is devoid of the fear of God.

There is one other key Old Testament passage for us to consider: Malachi 3. The chapter begins with the announcement of the coming of the one called the messenger of the covenant, a reference to our Lord Jesus Christ Himself. When He comes, the prophet says He will have a twofold ministry. First, it will be a ministry of purification:

"But who can endure the day of His coming?
And who can stand when He appears?
For He is like a refiner's fire
And like launderers' soap.
He will sit as a refiner and a purifier of silver;
He will purify the sons of Levi,
And purge them as gold and silver,
That they may offer to the LORD
An offering in righteousness." (Mal. 3:2–3)

Second, the messenger of the covenant will have a ministry of judgment:

"And I will come near you for judgment;
I will be a swift witness
Against sorcerers,
Against adulterers,
Against perjurers,
Against those who exploit wage earners and widows
    and orphans,
And against those who turn away an alien—
Because they do not fear Me,"
Says the LORD of hosts. (Mal. 3:5)

The messenger will come not only to purify but also to judge. Notice who is going to be judged: the sorcerers, adulterers, perjurers, those who exploit wage earners and widows and orphans, and those who "turn away an alien." In other words, the Lord says His judgment will come against all those found anywhere along the whole spectrum of evil, from those who are guilty of open, gross immorality to those who are indifferent to the needs of the sojourner. Then He points out that they have one thing in common:

"They do not fear Me." What does the adulterer have in common with the person who is indifferent to a legitimate need in another human being that he has the capacity to meet if only he had the will to do so? According to this text, the common denominator is that they do not walk in the fear of God. So the prophet Malachi tells us that God's judgment will come forth with fury and vengeance on all who do not fear Him.

Religious Hypocrites

The passages already cited deal primarily with those who are openly irreligious in their wickedness, but there is another great class of persons who have no fear of God. It is those who are very religious outwardly, but who are guilty of religious hypocrisy. They maintain an outward profession of true religion and perform many of its activities, but they are devoid of the power of true religion. The classic example of such a class of people is the scribes and the Pharisees.

In Matthew 6, our Lord called the scribes and Pharisees hypocrites and warned us not to be like them. The reason is, He argued, when they pray, they pray to be seen by men (v. 5); when they give, they give to be seen by men (v. 2); and when they fast, they fast to be seen by men (v. 16). That is, in all their effort to maintain the form of orthodox religion and in all their religious activities, they are devoid of the fear of God. For what is the essence of the fear of God? It is the regard of His person that makes His smile my greatest delight and His frown my greatest dread. It is that which makes me a man or woman who desires nothing beyond my own conscience for a theater and God for a witness. To that, the scribes and Pharisees were strangers.

Professing Christian, where is your heart? Men can see you go through the motions of devotion to God and obedience to His commands. But the question is, what does God see? Does He see that your outward conformity to His law is an expression of the fear of God in your heart? Does He see that you worship Him out of love to Him and out of a desire to please Him, constrained by the awareness of your obligations to Him? Or have your religious activities simply become a routine part of your lifestyle, in which you remain so that you "may be seen of men"?

Why do you do what you do? Why don't you do some of the things other people do? Is it simply to keep up the form and semblance of true religion before the eyes of men? Jesus said to the scribes and Pharisees, "Even so you also outwardly appear righteous to men, but inside you are full of hypocrisy and lawlessness" (Matt. 23:28). The person who maintains orthodox religion in the head and the form of it in his life but who is a stranger to the fear of God in the heart knows nothing of the inwardness of true, saving, biblical Christianity. He knows nothing of poverty of spirit. He knows nothing of hungering and thirsting after righteousness. He knows nothing of mourning over his sins in secret. The sum and substance of his whole religious experience is what is packed into his head and what he performs outwardly in his life; but of the going forth of a heart after God, he knows nothing.

This absence of the fear of God is exerting a profound influence on our whole culture at this point in history.

Suppose I were legally authorized to demolish an old deserted house sitting on a vacant lot. There are two main ways I could go about it. I could arm myself with the necessary tools and, beginning on the roof, start tearing the house down piece by piece—shingle by shingle, brick by brick, door by door. But there is another way I could do it. I could take my sledge hammer and start working on the foundation. After an hour's time a passerby might not be able to see what I was trying to do. The house would still look completely intact. All I may have been able to accomplish is to displace a few concrete blocks or put a hole in the poured concrete foundation. At the end of the day the house might still be standing if I am taking the second approach to destroying it, whereas someone up on the roof could have made quite a mess during the time I was pounding away at the foundation. He could have some of the sheathing on the roof torn off. He might have some of the windows knocked out. But if I stick with it, by the end of two or three days, I would be a lot farther ahead than he would be. If I could undercut the strategic points of stress where the foundation bore the weight of that whole structure, I could bring the whole house down upon itself, whereas at the end of a couple of days, just working piece by piece, the other man might leave 80 percent of the structure still standing.

The devil hates the structure of biblical ethics and morality wherever he sees that structure raised. There are two ways he can go about to destroy it. He can start attacking every shingle of Christian virtue and say, "There is no such thing as sexual purity, and I'm out to destroy the concept of such purity. There is no such thing as honesty, and

I'm going to start tearing away at the shingles of honesty." But the devil is smarter than that. He says, "Go ahead and keep your shingles for a while. Let everybody walk by and see them still intact. What I'm going to do is to go around back where you can't see me, and I am going to start dislodging the concrete foundation blocks."

What has happened in our own Western culture? What has happened in America? For several generations the devil has been out back, working at the foundations. One of his great hammer blows was that of religious liberalism, which distorted the God of the Bible and turned Him from the glorious, fearful God of Israel, the God and Father of our Lord Jesus Christ, into a formless mass of unprincipled sentiment called love. His holiness, justice, and righteous anger were largely forgotten if not flatly denied. Then there was the hammer blow of humanism that came through our public education system. It taught that man is not a depraved and natively sinful creature with a strong and powerful internal bias toward evil. And there was the hammer blow of evolutionary thought: Man is not obligated to God because he never came from the creative hand of God in the first place—the primordial slime finds it difficult to codify a system of ethics! If men and women are told that they are really nothing more than sophisticated animals, should it surprise us if they eventually act like animals?

All of these influences have been at work demolishing the foundation for ethics so that the house that looked beautiful yesterday is in shambles today. Everyone says, "Look, the house is falling down on us!" Why? It is because the fear of God has essentially vanished from the fabric of our national life and experience. The only way there will be any widespread return to biblical ethics and morality is to start from the beginning by implanting the fear of God in the hearts of people. That is where such a return must begin; and it is only the gospel of God's saving grace in the person and work of Jesus Christ applied by the Holy Spirit that can construct this foundation of the fear of God in the hearts of people.

This means we must go back to telling people who God is as our creator, lawgiver, and judge and about the ethical and moral standards He requires of His creatures. When they begin to see who He is and what He requires of them, they will begin to see how terrible it is to sin against and to offend such a holy God, until they are driven to despair. Then, when they are told that this holy God, who could justly damn us all, so loved the world that He gave His only begotten Son, they will see forgiveness from the perspective of the psalmist: "But there is forgiveness with You, that You may be feared" (Ps. 130:4). The gospel will no longer be converted into a cheap elixir that puts people at ease with their own sinful conduct while doing nothing to promote the fear of God. Rather, the proclamation of a robust biblical gospel with its call to repentance and radical discipleship will be the instrument by which, through the blessings of the new covenant applied in power to the heart and conscience, men and women, boys and girls will be brought to fear and to reverence this God while rejoicing in His free and full forgiveness of their sins. This work of God will then find expression as it causes those who experience its power to walk in His precepts and commandments with a heart filled with joy and love to this gracious God and Savior.

Testimony of the Unbeliever

The absence of the fear of God explains not only the spiritual condition of our nation but also the behavior of every individual who is devoid of this fear. Why does the unbeliever live the way he lives? Why does the unbelieving young person get up in the morning, eat, go off to school, lie a little bit, cheat a little bit, fight with his brother and sister, and hide the truth from his parents? Here is the explanation. There is no fear of God before his eyes. It is the explanation of the lives of unbelieving adults as well.

Sadly, this is why many who profess to be followers of Christ can go home from church on a Lord's Day and during afternoon and evening turn on their TV sets without even thinking whether or not what they purpose to watch is in any way consistent with the command of God to "remember the Sabbath day to keep it holy." They think that how they spend the Lord's Day is *their* business, not God's. They cannot stand to think that God may have something to say about what they should do or not do on a Lord's Day afternoon. That is their attitude. Why? Because on that issue at that time when they are deciding what they should or should not do on His day, there is no fear of God before their eyes.

Dear reader, if an honest review of the patterns of your life reveals that the fear of God does not form the foundational framework for your existence, you need to recognize that until you come to Jesus and have Him implant this fear within your heart, this will continue to be your life's pattern. Dying in that state, you will experience why the Lord Jesus commanded men to "fear Him who is able to destroy both soul and body in hell" (Matt. 10:28).

Questions for Reflection and Discussion

1. What are the two propositions that constitute the substance of this chapter?

2. Who are the two Old Testament characters highlighted in this chapter whose experience illustrates that the fear of God is the foundation of godly behavior? Specifically, how did the fear of God function in them when facing moral and ethical choices?

3. What are several specific ways in which the fear of God should influence your own ethical behavior?

4. How has the absence of the fear of God manifested itself in our life as a nation?

5. Do we have the power to implant the fear of God in the hearts of our children? Does their failure to walk in the fear of God automatically indicate that there has been basic parental failure in teaching and manifesting the fear of God? Explain.

6. How did the absence of the fear of God shape the religious thinking and practice of the scribes and the Pharisees?

7. How does true revival alter the moral and social fabric of any given community that God may visit with an outpouring of His Spirit?

8. What is the key text which traces ungodly living to the absence of the fear of God?

◆

CHAPTER SIX

How to Maintain and Increase the Fear of God

In this study, we have seen that the fear of God is one of the most basic themes of Holy Scripture. Yet sadly, in our day, in many religious circles it is one of the most neglected themes of Scripture. John Murray wrote the statement I used in the opening words of this book—that "the fear of God is the soul of godliness."[1] In other words, there is no life of godliness unless it is continually animated by the soul of the fear of God. We have seen that Scripture warrants the conclusion that the fear of God is the soil out of which a godly life grows, and the absence of the fear of God is the soil out of which an ungodly life grows. Because this subject is so vital, we need to consider some very practical instruction concerning how we are to maintain and increase the fear of God in our hearts.

A basic text that helps put this subject into perspective is Proverbs 23:17. In this portion of Scripture we are given, first, a negative command: "Do not let your heart

---

1. Murray, *Principles of Conduct*, 229.

envy sinners" (v. 17a). Don't allow your heart to begin to be jealous of the dainties of the ungodly. Don't allow your spirit to begin to be affected with any kind of longing for what they call life's pleasures, "but be zealous for the fear of the LORD all the day" (v. 17b). In other words, the opposite of a heart that goes out with envy toward sinners and their sinful course of life is a heart that maintains a proper and ever-present sense of the fear of God.

How do we maintain the fear of God in our hearts? That it is God's will that we maintain the fear of God in our hearts is beyond dispute in the light of the text just quoted. We have an explicit command to maintain it, even "all the day." In answer to the question, *how* do we do this, we will first consider a general principle that is the foundation for the answer. Then we will consider eight specific guidelines for maintaining and increasing in the fear of God.

The Foundational Principle

First, there is a general principle that we must understand and learn to live by if we are to maintain and increase the fear of God in our hearts. Simply stated, that principle is this: When it comes to living the Christian life, *the focus of our conscious spiritual endeavors is to be the very things God declares to be the result of His own work in us*.

Let me seek to explain and illustrate this vital principle. Galatians 5:22–23 states that "the fruit of the Spirit is love, joy, peace, longsuffering, kindness, goodness, faithfulness, gentleness, self-control. Against such there is no law." Whenever you see a person who manifests genuine, selfless, Christian love, you must attribute the source of that love to a deep, powerful, inward work of the Holy Spirit. The fruit of the Spirit is love. This means that love is the manifestation of the Holy Spirit's presence and work. Wherever you see genuine joy and peace and these other Christian graces, you are seeing the work of the Holy Spirit. This is beyond dispute. If we have any acquaintance with Scripture and our own hearts, we know that these graces are only brought into the life and only flow out of the life by the work of the Holy Spirit in us.

However, the same God who tells us that these graces are the fruit of His working in us also informs us through the same apostle in Colossians 3:12, "Therefore, as the elect of God, holy and beloved, *put on* tender mercies, kindness, humility, meekness, longsuffering." Then He says in verse 14, "But above all these things *put on* love." The Bible asserts that love is the fruit of the Spirit, and it is God's work to produce it; yet at the same time, it tells *us* to put it on. And "put on" is a verb of action. You did not lie in bed this morning and wait for your clothes to come out of your closet, make their way to your bed, and crawl onto your body. You had to get up and go to them, pick them up, and put them on yourself. Putting on is a personal, conscious activity.

Now, which is it? Is the presence of love and meekness in the life of a Christian the work of God, or is it the work of the believer? The answer is that it is not *either/or*, but *both*. The fruit of the Spirit is love—put on love. And the same thing is true with all these other graces. The fruit of the Spirit is joy, and yet Philippians 4:4 says, "Rejoice in the Lord always. Again I will say, rejoice!"

This principle I am attempting to explain is most beautifully and precisely stated in Philippians 2:12–13, where Paul says, "Therefore, my beloved, as you have always obeyed, not as in my presence only, but now much more in my absence, work out your own salvation with fear and trembling; for it is God who works in you both to will and to do for His good pleasure." That is, apply yourself consciously and diligently to the outworking of God's saving purposes in your life, with particular reference to the development of these graces that constitute a blameless life. Yet the command for us to "work out" is based on the certainty of God's working in us. God's working does not negate the necessity of our working, and our working does not cancel out the reality and efficacy of His working. They are coextensive and confluent in the life of the believer.

It is essential to understand this principle if we are to maintain and increase the fear of God in our hearts. Putting the fear of God into the heart of anyone is declared to be a sovereign work of God as a promised blessing of the new covenant (Jer. 32:40). It is one of the saving blessings God has imparted to His elect in all ages in conjunction with their conversion. In light of this, someone could reason that if it is God's work to put His fear in our hearts, then the way to increase the fear of God is obvious—you've just got to pray and trust that the Lord will do it. But that is not how it works. The principle is this: *What God declares to be His work in us is to be the focus of our conscious labors and endeavors.*

In our efforts to be directed by the Word of God, we must not allow the possible accusations of legalism and moralism to scare us away from seeking to discover in

Scripture the specific guidelines that God has given us by which we may develop and increase the fear of God in our hearts. It both vexes and amazes me that in an age of blatant lawlessness and antinomianism so many seem to be scared of anything that could even begin to look like legalism and moralism, as though these two realities were our greatest practical danger! Someone once asked a Puritan why he lived such a precise life in which he had constant regard to the precepts and principles of Scripture touching every facet of his life. He answered, "Sir, you ask me why I live a precise life? My answer is simple. I serve a precise God." Why should we be concerned with discovering specific rules and guidelines for maintaining the fear of God? Because the God who has made us and before whom we walk has given us these principles in order that we might know how better to increase His fear in our hearts.

The conscious, deliberate effort of the child of God is not necessarily to be regarded as self-effort in the sense that he is negating the necessity for the grace of God. No, God alone can put His fear into our hearts. He is working in us to will and to do His good pleasure. But we must work out with fear and trembling the cultivation and development of that fear in the context of abiding in Christ and depending on the work of the Holy Spirit.

Specific Directives for Maintaining the Fear of God

That brings us to the second area of our consideration. Having stated and explained the general principle, now we come to the specific directives for maintaining and increasing the fear of God in our hearts.

An Interest in the New Covenant

The first directive is *be certain that you have an interest in the new covenant.* I use the term "interest" not to refer to mere curiosity or concern about something, but in its primary meaning of "having a share or a participation in something." In this sense, if someone says he has an interest in a specific retail business, he does not mean that he goes by once in a while and looks at the shop window. It means he has invested time, energy, and money in that business.

Scripture tells us that the presence of the fear of God in the heart is the result of God's work in fulfilling one of the promises of the new covenant. As we have previously discovered, in Jeremiah 32:40, God says, "I will put My fear in their hearts." As long as you are a stranger to the blessings of the new covenant, Paul's description of the ungodly in Romans 3:18 will continue to be your experience: "There is no fear of God before their eyes." Unless you come to God through Christ in repentance and faith, pleading no basis of your approach to God but the blood of the everlasting covenant shed for sinners, you will be characterized by the absence of the fear of God until you die. By nature no one fears God with the fear of veneration and awe that is always joined to the love of and trust in the gracious promises of God.

You may have that fear and dread of God that drives you from Him, but you don't have that biblical fear, that regard for God's character which draws your heart out to Him in love, trust, devotion, and a deep desire to please Him. You have a dread of God. You try to push thoughts of God out of your mind. You live your day-to-day life as though God did not exist. You may go into a building called a church once a week and go through the outward motions of worship. But you do not live in the fear of God. What God says in His Word about how you should live your life has no real, practical effect upon the thoughts, motives, words, and deeds that constitute the patterns of your life. There is no fear of God before your eyes. The reality of who God is and His claims over you are not the dominant, governing principle of your life.

That is true of every one of us by nature. If you are a Christian, no doubt you think back with shame on the years in which you lived that way. Just like the heathen who wrings off the head of his chicken and sprinkles a little blood on his altar, we may have (speaking in a metaphor) wrung the head off an hour or two a week and sprinkled it at the foot of some altar in some church. We gave a little time and a little money, but we lived totally devoid of the fear of God until God arrested us by His grace and put His fear within our hearts.

Thus, if you would know the increase of the fear of God, you must first be certain that you have come to Jesus Christ, the Mediator of the new covenant. Hebrews 12:22a and 24 say of all true believers that "you have come…to Jesus the Mediator of the new covenant." It is only as we come to Him with the disposition of the hymn writer— "Nothing in my hands I bring, simply to Thy cross I cling"—that He will make good in us all the blessings of that covenant that He sealed with His own precious blood.

Child of God, do you long for an increase of the fear of God? Then make your interest in the new covenant the solid ground on which you stand when you plead for an increase of His fear. When you pray, "Oh, God, increase Thy fear in me," the argument you ought to press before God should be that Jesus Christ has died as the Mediator of the new covenant, and that one of the blessings promised in that covenant is that God would put His fear into your heart. Pray, "Lord Jesus, on the basis of Thy shed blood I plead for an increase of Thy fear. Give me as much of Thy fear as the blood of the covenant warrants and has secured for me."

The Scriptures

Second, if you would sustain and increase your fear of God, you must *feed your mind on the Scriptures in general.* Psalm 19 celebrates the excellence of the two great books of divine revelation. Verses 1 to 6 celebrate the revelation of Himself that God has made in creation: "The heavens declare the glory of God; and the firmament shows His handiwork" (v. 1). Verses 7 to 11 celebrate the revelation God has made in His Word: "The law of the LORD is perfect" (v. 7). According to these texts, God has given us two books in which He has made a disclosure of Himself: the book of creation and the book of written Scripture. These two books are generally designated as general revelation and special revelation.

Notice in particular what David does as he praises God for His special revelation, beginning with verse 7. He says, "The law of the LORD is perfect, converting the soul." Then he uses another term: "The testimony of the LORD is sure, making wise the simple." Another term is used in verse 8: "The statutes of the LORD are right, rejoicing the heart"; and another, "The commandment of the LORD is pure, enlightening the eyes." Finally, in the last part of verse 9, he says, "The judgments of the LORD are true and righteous altogether." Now, notice, in the midst of all these tributes to the Word of God, in which David uses these various terms to describe special revelation, what he says in the first part of verse 9: "The fear of the LORD is clean, enduring forever." What is the point? David is asserting that there is an inseparable relationship between the special revelation God has made in Scripture and the fear of God. And this relationship is such that, for all intents and purposes, the fear of God can be used as a synonym for the Word of God. This is why David can so freely insert "the fear of the Lord" in a parallel relationship to all of these terms referring to God's Word. What does that tell us? It tells us that he who would increase in the fear of God must feed his mind on the Scriptures in general. The Word of the Lord is so productive of the fear of the Lord that the two things may be used synonymously.

This is why when a present, vital, consistent, and extensive relationship to the Scriptures begins to wane, the roots of the fear of God will begin to shrivel. You will grow no more in the fear of God than you grow in your understanding and assimilation of the written Word of God. It is a daily necessity that you expose yourself to the Scriptures as much as possible, both in private and in the family circle. It is also necessary that you faithfully and regularly attend the public reading, singing, preaching, and teaching of the Word of God (Col. 3:16). Though there are many portions of Scripture that, as far as we can discern, may have no direct influence in the sustaining and increasing of the fear of God, the overall effect of every truth of Scripture is to feed the fear of God. In one way or another, the individual who absorbs the most Scripture, spiritually assimilating it into his heart, life, and very being, is the one who will know most of the fear of God.

When you are tempted to cut corners on those disciplines by which you are exposing your mind to Scripture, remember that such a decline is part of the subtle effort of the devil to move you away from the sanctifying influence of the fear of God. A move away from the fear of God always precedes a departure from godliness, as we saw in the previous chapter. If you and I are to be moved out of the path of godliness, we must first abandon, to some degree, the fear of God. Often the first step to abandoning His fear is cutting corners on either or both our private and public exposure to the Word of God.

If we succumb to this temptation, we must not be surprised if in the crucible of a specific enticement to sin, when the pressure is on and God's smile or God's frown ought to be the all-important issue, that somehow those great spiritual realities seem very distant. There is not a Christian who has lived a year as a true child of God who will not confess that there are times when God and Christ and heaven and hell and judgment and godliness can all seem so remote and little more than words and theories. Isn't it true? Sometimes you ask yourself, "Who in the world am I? What in the world do I believe? How can these things really be a part of me and seem so distant from me?" The answer is often, though not always, very simple—it is because there has been an erosion of systematic, consistent exposure to and assimilation of the Word of God.

It is not as though you came to a certain day and said, "All right, from this day forward, the Bible and I will have nothing to do with each other." It wasn't like that at all. There was just a little extra pressure that made you cut corners on your set time with God. Just a few extra responsibilities one day and a few added distractions the next day, until, after a week or two, you no longer keenly felt the fruit of neglecting your Bible. You were no longer painfully aware of the erosion. Then there was the tragic breakdown in your Christian life and experience, to the extent that one day you said, "When did it all happen?" The answer is that it happened as the result of your gradual alienation from the Word of God. I know no shortcut to maintaining the fear of God. Therefore, the second guideline to maintaining and increasing in the fear of God is that you must consistently, systematically, and prayerfully feed your mind and heart with Scripture. The Scriptures affirm unequivocally that "man shall not live by bread alone; but man lives by every word that proceeds from the mouth of the Lord" (Deut. 8:3).

The Forgiveness of God
Third, *feed your soul with the reality of the forgiveness of God.* In a key text we previously considered, the psalmist asked the question in Psalm 130:3: "If You, LORD, should mark iniquities, O Lord, who could stand?" It is an admission that if God were to record every sin ever committed and then summon sinners into His presence one by one to give Him an account, no one could stand before Him. The prospect

of a holy, omniscient God calling the creature to an account for every sin is enough to make one cry out, as many will cry in the day of judgment, that the rocks and the mountains might fall upon them (Rev. 6:15–17). One can only dread a God who marks sins and will call men into judgment for them. But, remarkably, the psalmist answers his own question by saying, "But there is forgiveness with You, that You may be feared" (Ps. 130:4). When we discover that this great God, holy and just and omniscient as He is, actually forgives sins, and that all of His glorious attributes have been fully engaged to grant me a just pardon and full acceptance, how can we help but fear Him "with deepest, tenderest fears; and worship Him with trembling hope, and penitential tears."[2] The psalmist is testifying that as his mind is filled with the wonder of forgiveness, so his heart is filled with the reality of the fear of God.

Thus will it be for you also. The measure to which the fact and wonder of forgiving grace sinks into your soul will be the measure of your fear of God. Feed often on the reality of God's forgiveness. God, who is holy; God, who is righteous; God, who is called the high and the lofty one—He actually forgives me, the sinful creature. Steep your mind often in this great and blessed truth of forgiveness. Why did the second person of the Godhead ever become flesh and dwell among us? Why should Deity be enclosed in a virgin's womb? Why should He be born in an animal shelter? Why should He die that shameful and horrific death

---

2. "My God, How Wonderful Thou Art," in *The Trinity Hymnal* (Philadelphia: Orthodox Presbyterian Church, 1961), 31.

on the cross? The answer to every one of these questions is in order that the sons of men might receive forgiveness in a way that is consistent with God's holiness, justice, and righteousness and with the demands of His inflexible law.

As we feed not only on the fact of forgiveness but also on the way of forgiveness, our fear of God will be deepened and increased. I would remind you of those perceptive words of Manton quoted earlier: "The heart is shy of a condemning God, but it adheres to a pardoning God. And nothing breeds this fear of God so much as a tender sense of God's goodness in Jesus Christ." Psalm 34:8 is a well-known text, often used as a gospel invitation. There, David says, "Oh taste and see that the Lord is good!" Then he says in verse 9, "Oh fear the Lord, you his saints." We cannot fear God as He ought to be feared except in the context of His abundant goodness and His condescending mercy in Jesus Christ. Therefore, if you would have the fear of God sustained in your heart, feed your soul on God's forgiveness. Don't allow yourself to go back under the terrors of the law that will drive you from Him.[3] Allow yourself to bask in the mystery of His forgiveness and stand amazed at such a display of grace—that it not only took hold of you when you were wallowing in your filth, but also bears so patiently with you in all of your wanderings and your

---

3. In giving this directive I am not in any way discouraging the proper use of the law (the Ten Commandments) as a gracious guide and definer of holiness. Any view of the law that makes us uncomfortable praying through Psalm 119 is not of God! Consult the book by Mark Jones entitled *Antinomianism: Reformed Theology's Unwelcome Guest?* (Phillipsburg, N.J.: P&R, 2013).

stumblings. Stand amazed before such a display of forgiveness, and the fear of God will flourish in your heart.

The Greatness of God

The fourth directive is *learn to feed your soul on the majestic greatness of God*. By that, I mean those aspects of His character and attributes such as His absolute sovereignty, holiness, power, omnipotence, and immensity. Notice this perspective in Revelation 15:3–4. In this particular vision, John sees a sea of glass and those who have triumphed in their conflict with the beast. John then describes them as engaged in singing the song of Moses and the song of the Lamb, comprised of these words:

> Great and marvelous are Your works,
> Lord God Almighty!
> Just and true are Your ways,
> O King of the saints!
> Who shall not fear You, O Lord, and glorify Your name?
> For You alone are holy.
> For all nations shall come and worship before You,
> For Your judgments have been manifested.

What attributes of God are in focus in this song? His greatness, holiness, power, righteousness, and sovereignty. What are these attributes, but those aspects of God that set before us the majesty of His greatness? And the heavenly choir says that as we contemplate His majestic greatness, it is unthinkable that any rational creature would not fear such a God. "Who shall not fear you, O Lord?" If a creature knows God as He is revealed, he cannot help but fear Him.

The principle for us as God's people is this: If you would grow in the fear of God, then you must feed your soul on the majestic greatness of God.

More specifically, become familiar with those portions of Scripture most calculated to set these realities before you. Periodically read through a passage such as Isaiah 40. That is the passage in which the prophet gives a lofty description of the majestic greatness of God and pulls together imagery such as is seldom to be found in any literature. He speaks of the entire expanse of the heavens being but the span of God's hand. He says all the nations are like a drop of condensation on the side of a bucket. He speaks of all the multitudes of the nations as a swarming mass of grasshoppers. He thinks of God as a great shepherd and all the galaxies and all the stars as sheep, each of which He calls by name. Such beautiful imagery! What is it all there for? It is there to impress on us the greatness of our God. The chapter begins with the command to the messengers of Judah to get up into a high mountain and to say to the cities of Judah, "Behold your God." Look on Him. Fix your gaze on Him as He is revealed. We should be familiar with such portions of Scripture as Isaiah 40 and Revelation 1.

We should also attach ourselves to a church and ministry that will assist us to maintain lofty views of God. Negatively stated, flee from a ministry that encourages in any way a casual and cavalier lovey-dovey relationship to the Deity. Such a disposition is an abomination to God. In our day, much that borders on being blasphemous is carried out in the name of worship because it deliberately seeks to promote such base and unworthy concepts of God. Attach yourself to a ministry that assists you to think of God in His majestic greatness. The hymn writer captured it well: "Majestic sweetness sits enthroned upon the Savior's brow."[4] Pure sweetness would degenerate into unprincipled sentiment. Pure majesty would be too intimidating to make us feel comfortable to draw near. But when you have majesty and sweetness together, you have the God of the Bible as He is revealed to us in Jesus Christ. Therefore, attach yourself to a ministry that assists you to feed your soul on His sweet but majestic greatness.

Also, read literature that will assist you to think often on His greatness. Many of the more popular Christian books published in our own day are "how-to" books or books in which each author is committed to "telling his or her story." One can visit many Christian bookstores and scour their shelves in vain seeking to find books that will set before you how great, majestic, and exalted our great triune God is. On the other hand, we all ought to be filled with gratitude to God that there are many bookstores today whose shelves are weighed down with biblically weighty books that promote weighty views of God and His ways.

We should be deeply grateful to God for writers whom He has raised up in recent years to think large thoughts of God and convey those thoughts in their writings. I am thinking of authors and their books such as J. I. Packer's *Knowing God*; A. W. Pink's *The Sovereignty of God*; R. C. Sproul's *The Holiness of God*; John Murray's *Redemption Accomplished and Applied*; J. C. Ryle's reprinted book *Holi-*

---

4. "Majestic Sweetness Sits Enthroned," in *The Trinity Hymnal*, 143.

ness; Jerry Bridges's *Trusting God*; and A. W. Tozer's *The Pursuit of God*—just to name a few.

Until the relatively recent revival of interest in historic Reformed theology, you would have had to go back to earlier generations of writers to find the kind of literature that would help you to think of the greatness and the majesty of God. When Christians read old books, it is not just because they are antiquarians. It is because they find there the writings of men whose souls were permeated with the sense of the majestic greatness of God. And when we enter into those pages, we somehow sense we are breathing the rarified air of the biblical thoughts of who God really is.

Thankfully, we now have access to many of the classic Puritan works of authors such as Owen, Flavel, Manton, Goodwin, Charnock, Sibbes, Brooks, Bunyan, and others. Many of the original works of these authors have been condensed, updated into modern and accessible English, and made available very inexpensively by means of various digital devices.

Further, acquaint yourselves with hymnody that reflects the majesty of God. For a number of years, my family and I would sing and memorize hymns while driving to our church building. I quote the hymn by Frederick Faber which helped us to think high thoughts of our God.

> My God, how wonderful thou art,
> Thy majesty how bright!
> How beautiful thy mercy seat,
> In depths of burning light!
>
> How dread are thine eternal years,
> O everlasting Lord,

By holy angels, day and night,
Incessantly adored!

O how I fear thee, living God,
With deepest, tend'rest fears;
And worship thee with trembling hope,
And penitential tears.

Yet I may love thee too, O Lord,
Almighty as thou art;
For thou hast stooped to ask of me
The love of my poor heart.

No earthly father loves like thee,
No mother half so mild
Bears and forbears as thou hast done
With me, thy sinful child.

How wonderful, how beautiful,
The sight of thee will be,
Thine endless wisdom, boundless power,
And aweful purity!

Father of Jesus, love's reward,
What rapture will it be,
Prostrate to lie before thy throne,
And gaze and gaze on thee.[5]

Awareness of God's Presence

The fifth practical directive for increasing our experience of the fear of God is *seek to cultivate an awareness of God's presence.* "Be zealous for the fear of the LORD all the day" (Prov.

---

5. "My God, How Wonderful Thou Art," in *The Trinity Hymnal*, 31.

23:17). Since the day is made up of hours spent in the home, car, school, playground, ball field, office, and many other places, it is in those places that we must cultivate the awareness of God's presence. A passage that sets out very well just how this is done is Psalm 16:8: "I have set the LORD always before me." David is saying that in every situation, he places God before him so that he realizes in that situation he is in the very presence of God.

You may ask, What does this mean and exactly how do we set God before us? I answer with the following scenario. A Christian student enters his classroom saying to himself, "As I enter this classroom I acknowledge that I do so before the face and in the presence of my Savior God. God is right here in this classroom with all these kids that don't give a hoot about my God or about my standards. He is here to be loved, honored, confessed, and obeyed at any cost. I have set the Lord before me." For this reason I will not cheat in taking the exam that is placed on my desk. The wicked don't do this. David says they do not set God before themselves (Ps. 54:3). They set their own lust before them. They set their own ambitions before them. They set their own flexible standards before them, but they don't set God before them. To walk in God's fear is to cultivate this awareness of His presence. You cannot fear a distant and a forgotten God. If God is feared, it is as a God who is near and who is remembered.

Practically speaking, this means we ought often to meditate on Psalm 139 and the truths it declares. Do you want to cultivate the awareness of God's presence? Make it a frequent practice to read, pray over, and pray in Psalm 139 often. "Where can I go from Your Spirit? Or where can I flee from Your presence? If I ascend into heaven, You are there; if I make my bed in hell, behold, You are there" (vv. 7–8). These verses capture David's sense of the pervasiveness of God's presence. Seek to remind yourself in every situation that God is there. You must learn to do this. You can't just pray, "Lord, please do this for me." The psalmist says, "*I have set* the LORD always before me." David is describing a discipline which had become a fixed spiritual habit. That possibility stands open to you as well. God is there. David's setting Him there did not put Him there; He was already there. But it is the recognition that He is there that becomes the transforming experience in our lives. May God therefore help us to cultivate this awareness of His presence.

Consciousness of Obligation to God
The sixth rule is *seek to cultivate the consciousness of your obligations to God.* As we saw in our description of the fear of God, one indispensable element of it is that in each situation the Christian realizes that his relationship to God is the most important relationship he has. The Christian college student may be taking an exam and may come to a point at which he realizes that the only way he can get a passing grade would be to cheat. But he says to himself that there is something more important than his relationship to his grades and to his parents who are paying his tuition—and that is his relationship to the God who has told him, "You shall not steal." That means, he understands, that he must not steal someone else's answer. If you are walking in the fear of God, before you leave for school in the morning,

you will say, "Lord, help me this day to walk in Thy fear." Then, when you are tempted to cheat, the recognition of your obligation to God will be stronger than the recognition of your obligation to present an impressive, but dishonest, report card to show your father and mother.

It means that when your lust and passions cry out and would dictate a course of action contrary to the law of God, if necessary you will stick your heel into the face of your lust in order that you may be able to look up unashamed into the face of your God. Joseph's words will now become your words: "How then can I do this great wickedness, and sin against God?" (Gen. 39:9).

A time may come in your life where the desires of your parents or other close relatives may be found in a collision course with the will of God for your life. The Lord says, even if you must sever deep earthly ties, do it—for, He says, "Do not think that I came to bring peace on earth. I did not come to bring peace but a sword. For I have come to 'set a man against his father, a daughter against her mother, and a daughter-in-law against her mother-in-law'; and 'a man's enemies will be those of his own household'" (Matt. 10:34–36).

In speaking these words, our Lord was telling us, "I came to implant the blessings of the new covenant in the hearts of men so that they will fear Me to the extent that, even if they must sever the deepest of earthly ties, they will be willing to do it for My sake." He said that is what He came to do. And that is what occurs when the people of God cultivate a consciousness of their supreme obligations to Him.

Association with Those Who Fear God

If you would maintain and grow in your fear of God, the seventh guideline is *associate closely with those who walk in the fear of God.* While we are in this world, we must of necessity have dealings with those who don't fear God. Paul makes this clear in 1 Corinthians 5:9–10, when he says, "I wrote to you in my epistle not to keep company with sexually immoral people. Yet I certainly did not mean with the sexually immoral people of this world, or with the covetous, or extortioners, or idolaters, since then you would need to go out of the world." You cannot avoid having contact with those who don't fear God in the course of living a normal and productive life. You must have at least guarded and oftentimes surface relationships with the ungodly to live responsibly in this world and to establish bridges of friendship with a view to bearing witness to the truths of the gospel. But Paul means that where you have the opportunity and privilege to select your intimate friends, they ought to be God-fearing people. Psalm 119:63 is a key text in this regard: "I am a companion of all who fear You, and of those who keep Your precepts." The psalmist is telling us that he has deliberately chosen as his closest associates those whose fear of God is real and evident to any impartial observer.

Why did he do this? The psalmist understood the psychology of personal relationships. There is a power of imitation, absorption, and contagion between individuals, so that, all other things being equal, you will become like your most intimate associates. It is a law of nature, if you will. That is why Scripture says, "Make no friendship with an angry man, and with a furious man do not go, lest you learn his ways and set a snare for your soul" (Prov. 22:24–25). That is why God warns us against forming intimate associations with evil men—so that we don't become like them. This reality is what precipitated Paul's warning to the Corinthians: "Do not be deceived: 'Evil company corrupts good habits'" (1 Cor. 15:33). It is part of the way God has made us. We are not encased in our own individualism. God has ordained that men should live in community, and one of the inevitable byproducts of that arrangement is this built-in power of imitation, absorption, and contagion.

It is in this light that the psalmist said, "I am a companion of all who fear You." "Lord," he is saying, "I would fear Thee. And I know that one of the best ways to have Thy fear increased in my heart is to become the intimate associate of others who obviously fear Thee."

There is a wonderful commentary and illustration of this principle recorded in Malachi 3. In this passage, God indicts the great majority in Israel who have turned away from Him and are not giving Him His just due in terms of their offerings and sacrifices. It is a period of decadence in which God sounds forth the note of judgment. Yet in the midst of this nasty state of affairs, in verse 16, the prophet says, "Then those who feared the LORD spoke to one another, and the LORD listened and heard them; so a book of remembrance was written before Him for those who fear the LORD and who meditate on His name."

Here is a description of the godly remnant, that nucleus of true Israel, described as *those who feared the Lord* and meditated on His name. And because they were in the minority, they recognized the necessity of being sustained in their fear of God by seeking out others who feared Him. They needed to band together in the midst of the surrounding spiritual decadence. The judgments of God were being pronounced; decadence was on every side; and those who feared God were getting together and encouraging one another in the fear of God in the midst of that spiritual decay.

If you desire to grow in the fear of God, you must associate yourself closely with those who walk in His fear. No Christian grows and develops the graces of the Spirit in isolation. There is no such thing as a freelance Christianity and a do-it-yourself holiness. If you don't know and sense and feel how much you need your Christian brethren, you are living in a fool's paradise. You are undoubtedly guilty of indulging a delusive spirit of pride and self-confidence. As these godly people in the days of Malachi looked out and saw the corruption on every side and knew something of God's fear in their hearts, each one reasoned, "I'll go under if I try to make it by myself. Let me find others who fear Him, and we will speak often one to another."

What a cursed thing to be deluded into thinking you can make it on your own. God may have to humble you with a tragic and serious fall to get you to see that the body of Christ is not a luxury for your spiritual development. The church is not a frill. It is not an option if you desire to grow in grace. It is God's necessary place of growth and development. The basic thrust of a chapter such as 1 Corinthians 12 is that to every man is given a manifestation of the Spirit to profit all. The whole idea of Ephesians 4:1–16 is that the spiritual health and development of each individual member of the body of Christ is realized in the setting of the corporate life of the people of God. Each member supplies something to the body, and through that the body is built up more and "to the measure of the stature of the fullness of Christ" (Eph. 4:13).

Many professing Christians today relate to the people of God and the church the way people in the world relate to one another in so-called common law marriages. It has become an accepted thing for couples to live together outside of the bonds of marriage, designating their relationship as being "partners." In past generations, such a practice was looked on as immoral and shameful. But now it has become acceptable, to the point that many even think that marriage as an institution is unnecessary and passé. One of the terrible things about common law relationships is the philosophy that undergirds them. Whether they will admit it or not, the driving motive most people have who enter such relationships is their desire to have all the privileges of marriage with none of its binding responsibilities, inescapable commitments, and flesh-withering obligations. A man wants to share a bed and then breakfast with a woman, but the moment something develops that requires him to share *himself* with her in a way that will cost him something, he wants out, and he doesn't desire any inconvenience or expense connected with obtaining a divorce.

Similarly, many Christians are that way with respect to covenantal church membership. They want all the privileges of church membership and the fellowship of the people of God—a sound ministry of the word, an atmosphere where God is exalted and they are truly loved and accepted—but they don't want to be so bound that they can't conveniently slip out the moment the going gets rough. Are you a "common law" Christian? Or are you married, not only to Christ, but also to His people? If you are married to the people of God, and you have entered into a covenantal life with them, then when the first problem arises, you will not go your separate way.

That is one of the great blessings of the institution of marriage that is formalized civilly and publicly. Many of us will confess that we have faced many snags and difficulties working toward true marital intimacy. If we hadn't been bound by some deeper ties than simply an unwritten agreement that we would share the same roof and bed, we would no doubt have been tempted to run away from the relationship. However, it was the tight ties of a covenant of commitment, solemnly expressed in vows made before the face of God, that kept the relationship intact. Do you desire to grow in the fear of God? If you do, then associate yourself—intimately, not loosely—with those who walk together in His fear in covenantal church membership.

Fervent Prayer

The eighth and last word of counsel as to how we may grow in the fear of God is so obvious that perhaps some would even question the necessity for addressing it: *fervently pray for an increase of the fear of God.* One of the unalterable laws of God's kingdom is, "Ask, and it will be given to you" (Matt. 7:7). Or to put it negatively, as James did, "You do not have because you do not ask" (James 4:2).

When we begin to take seriously all that the Bible teaches us concerning the nature, efficacy, and place which prayer is to have in our lives, we find ourselves wrestling with some very profound issues. On the one hand, we know that our Bibles teach us that prayer must never be looked on as a spiritual exercise in which we the creatures get God in a hammerlock, forcing Him to give us things that otherwise He would refuse us. On the other hand, we cannot escape the obvious truth of James 4:2, which clearly asserts that there are things God would otherwise give us but which we do not have because we do not pray for them.

Part of the answer to this vexing concern is found in 1 John 5:14–15, where the inspired apostle tells us, "Now this is the confidence that we have in Him, that if we ask anything according to His will, He hears us. And if we know that He hears us, whatever we ask, we know that we have the petitions that we have asked of Him."

In light of all that has been written in this book concerning the centrality of the fear of God in connection with saving religion, true godliness, acceptable worship, and a host of other related issues, there should be no question in our minds that it is the will of God for us to grow in this grace of the fear of God. Therefore, in light of these words of the apostle John, when we pray for an increase of the fear of God, we ought to pray with unshakable confidence that we are indeed asking for something that is in accord with God's will. Having this confidence, we can pray for this increase in the firm expectation that God will indeed hear and answer such prayer. Furthermore, God has even given us a model prayer in the words of Psalm 86:11. David prays with these words: "Unite my heart to fear Your name."

Questions for Reflection and Discussion

1. What is the foundational principle crucial to understanding the concerns of this chapter?

2. What text of Scripture is perhaps the most helpful in demonstrating this principle?

3. What are the eight specific directives for cultivating greater measures of the fear of God? Discuss each one, highlighting at least one supportive text for each guideline.

4. Is the conscious effort to cultivate the fear of God necessarily a form of mere "moralism"? If not, when does that effort become mere "moralism"?

◆

CHAPTER SEVEN

A Final Word to the Reader

In chapter 1, I sought to establish the crucial importance of the fear of God by giving a brief and selective survey of the witness of Scripture to the fear of God in all the major sections of biblical revelation, from Genesis to Revelation. However, when selecting key texts out of the epistles, I deliberately omitted making reference to the passage with which I purpose to bring the burden of this book to its conclusion. The text is Hebrews 12:18–29, with a special focus on verses 28 and 29. For the reader's convenience in meditation, I give the whole text:

> For you have not come to the mountain that may be touched and that burned with fire, and to blackness and darkness and tempest, and the sound of a trumpet and the voice of words, so that those who heard it begged that the word should not be spoken to them anymore. (For they could not endure what was commanded: "And if so much as a beast touches the mountain, it shall be stoned or shot with an arrow." And so terrifying was the sight that Moses said, "I am exceedingly afraid and trembling.") But you have come

to Mount Zion and to the city of the living God, the heavenly Jerusalem, to an innumerable company of angels, to the general assembly and church of the first-born who are registered in heaven, to God the Judge of all, to the spirits of just men made perfect, to Jesus the Mediator of the new covenant, and to the blood of sprinkling that speaks better things than that of Abel. See that you do not refuse Him who speaks. For if they did not escape who refused Him who spoke on earth, much more shall we not escape if we turn away from Him who speaks from heaven, whose voice then shook the earth; but now He has promised, saying, "Yet once more I shake not only the earth, but also heaven." Now this, "Yet once more," indicates the removal of those things that are being shaken, as of things that are made, that the things which cannot be shaken may remain. Therefore, since we are receiving a kingdom which cannot be shaken, let us have grace, by which we may serve God acceptably with reverence and godly fear. For our God is a consuming fire.

The entire book of Hebrews is, in a very real sense, a passionate pastoral endeavor to persuade the vacillating professing Hebrew Christians to press on in persevering faith and obedience that they might enter the full and final rest of eternal life. As the writer to the Hebrews is bringing his pastoral letter to a conclusion, he demonstrates in a very vivid way the contrast between the circumstances and substance of the giving of the old covenant under Moses and the circumstances and substance of the blessings given in the new covenant by Jesus. This contrast is clearly captured by comparing the words of verse 18 with verse 22. In verse 18 the writer says, "For you have *not* come to," while in verse 22 he says, "But you *have* come to."

He brings a final warning against the danger of refusing what God is saying to us in the person and work of Christ within the framework of the new covenant. This warning is framed within verses 25–27. Then, in verses 28–29, he sets before us a capstone exhortation in these words: "Therefore, since we are receiving a kingdom which cannot be shaken, let us have grace, by which we may serve God acceptably with reverence and godly fear. For our God is a consuming fire."[1]

The circumstances surrounding the giving of the old covenant were so terrifying that even Moses said, "I am exceedingly afraid and trembling" (v. 21). This was the fear of terror and dread—the fear from which the blessings of the new covenant are calculated, in great measure (though not completely), to deliver us. However, the blessings of God in the new covenant are not given to negate that fear of God which is "the soul of godliness" and is identified as one of the very blessings implanted in our hearts by virtue of the new covenant. Rather, according to verses 28–29, gratitude for all of the blessings conferred in the new covenant should move us to "serve [worship] God acceptably with reverence and godly fear. For our God is a consuming fire." If your professed acceptance of that salvation tendered to guilty sinners in Jesus Christ does not produce in you a disposition constraining you to worship God with reverence and godly

---

1. The verb rendered "serve" in some contexts is rightly rendered in others as "worship."

fear, something is radically defective in your thinking and professed experience of God's gracious salvation.

When we observe the patterns of much of the so-called "worship" carried on in our day by many who profess to be believers, we are forced to conclude that they have wrongly concluded that God is no longer a "consuming fire." It appears as though many "worship leaders" are committed to proving to us that God has morphed into a soft, pudgy, cuddly, little, foam-filled teddy bear. The writer to the Hebrews does not say that God *was a* consuming fire amid the smoke, blazing fire, and tempest and thunder of Mount Sinai. Rather, after enumerating the blessings of the new covenant, he declares that God yet "*is a* consuming fire." And it is this reality which is to shape all the contours of our worship and service rendered to Him.

The word "for" which ties verses 28 to 29 together indicates that the nature of our worship and service is determined by the nature of the God whom we worship and serve. Furthermore, the ethos and climate that should characterize the worship of the new covenant community is described as "reverence and godly fear." Contrary to the thinking of many, these words "reverence and godly fear" are *not* synonyms for morbidity, dryness, dullness, and dreariness.

Psalm 47:1–2, a Spirit-inspired call to worship, reads as follows: "Oh, clap your hands, all you peoples! Shout to God with the voice of triumph! For the LORD Most High is awesome; He is a great King over all the earth." In the mind of the psalmist, worship that is consistent with fearing God as the great king can be intensely exuberant, engaging the worshiper's heart, hands, and voice. Perhaps the seventeenth-century hymn writer Martin Rinkart had Psalm 47:1–2 in mind when he wrote these opening words to one of his hymns: "Now thank we all our God with *heart* and *hands* and *voices*."[2]

However, the words "reverence and godly fear" can in no way be made consistent with such things as calculated casualness, carnal flippancy, and jocularity, or that which is trite or tawdry. Furthermore, the words "reverence and godly fear" can never be made to square with prayers that are nothing more or less than quick little chit-chatty verbal approaches to the Deity that would never convey the idea that the God who is being addressed is not only "our Father in heaven" (Matt. 6:9), but that He is also the same God described by the prophet Isaiah as "the High and Lofty One who inhabits eternity, whose name is Holy" (Isa. 57:15), the very same God of Isaiah 6 before whom seraphim with veiled face and feet cry one to another, saying, "Holy, holy, holy is the LORD of hosts" (v. 3). We would all do well to listen to John Owen as he addresses the significance of worshipping "with reverence and godly fear." He writes:

> The sense of these words may be best learned from what they are opposed unto. Such as,
>
> 1. Want [lack] of a due sense of the majesty and glory of God with whom we have to do.
>
> 2. Want of a due sense of our own vileness.
>
> 3. Carnal boldness in a customary performance of

---

2. "Now Thank We All Our God," in *The Trinity Hymnal*, 86. Emphasis added.

sacred duties, which God abhors. Wherefore *reverence* is a holy abasement of soul in divine worship, in a sense of the majesty of God and our own vileness. And *godly fear* is a religious awe in the soul in holy duties, from a consideration of the great danger there is in sinful miscarriages in the worship of God.[3]

According to the clear biblical testimony, the church in Corinth was sovereignly blessed to possess many of those spiritual gifts unique to the apostolic age. In a congregation where those gifts were present and being regulated in their exercise by apostolic directives, it would be difficult to follow a wooden liturgical structure for a service of corporate worship and ministry. However, Paul assumes that in such a context of freedom and unusual manifestations of the Spirit of God, the concept of God conveyed through the exercise of these gifts would be such that the unbeliever or the uninstructed would have the secrets of his heart disclosed, and so, "falling down on his face, he will worship God and report that God is truly among you" (1 Cor. 14:24–25). In other words, that person whose mind was instructed by means of these unusual gifts is envisioned as coming to grips with the fact that the God who dwells in the midst of the gathered new covenant community is a God who is to be worshiped with "reverence and godly fear." The uninstructed or unbeliever is described as falling on his face and worshiping God. In that context, the uninstructed and the unbeliever are not led to believe that the God of the new covenant community is the snuggly little teddy bear of much of modern

---

3. John Owen, *Epistle to the Hebrews* (Grand Rapids: Kregel, 1968), 267.

evangelicalism—even of some in the so-called Reformed community—but that He is a God to be dealt with in a context of "reverence and awe."

It is only when individual Christians begin to take seriously the central place of the fear of God in biblically shaped Christian experience, that when they come together to render their worship, it will be characterized by "reverence and godly fear." May God be pleased to use the pages of this book to challenge many true believers to pursue an increased measure of that fear of God.

It is my prayer that some of you who have read these pages have come to the conclusion that, in your case, the total absence of the fear of God is an undeniable evidence that you have never experienced the manifold blessings of the salvation freely and sincerely offered to you in the gospel. My loving words of counsel and exhortation to you are very simple. Close this book, and go directly to Jesus, the Mediator of the new covenant. He stands ready to receive all who come to God by Him and to impart every single blessing promised to needy sinners in that covenant. In the language of the prophet Isaiah, I urgently entreat you: "Seek the LORD while He may be found, call upon Him while He is near. Let the wicked forsake his way, and the unrighteous man his thoughts; let him return to the LORD, and He will have mercy on him; and to our God, for He will abundantly pardon" (Isa. 55:6–7).

Questions for Reflection and Discussion

1. What passage of Scripture sets forth in the language of contrast the difference between the old and new covenants?

2. What is there in this passage that teaches us that the God who has established the new covenant is worthy of our reverence and awe?

3. What fundamental deficiency characterizes much of contemporary so-called worship? What is the root cause of this deficiency?

4. What should you do if you have come to the conviction through the reading of this book that your heart and life are completely devoid of any concrete evidence that you are a true God-fearer?